For online appendices, please go to www.scie.org.uk/
publications/adults.asp

Foreword

This report brings together the efforts of an energetic team from two organisations. The Foundation for People with Learning Disabilities and the Norah Fry Research Centre have combined their skills and long-term interests in how day services are developing to comment on best practice examples and to produce a literature search. The findings in the report are clear there is a fundamental shift taking place. Although slow in many places, there is a move away from people attending day centres five days weekly to more innovative and individualised participation in community activities.

While we were encouraged by many of the services we saw, some concerns emerged. Employment opportunities and effective transition planning remain underdeveloped, and more clarity about getting the best from adult and continuing education would be welcomed.

Two other issues concerned the team: a lack of options for people with high support needs particularly in the mainstream alongside non-disabled people and more specialist services for people from black and minority ethnic groups.

Many services are undergoing major changes. We look forward to hearing the lessons learnt and the new choices that will be on offer!

Barbara McIntosh
Co Director
Foundation for People with Learning Disabilities

Acknowledgements

The team would like to acknowledge the great contribution made by our late colleague, Ken Simons, in helping us all re-think the basis of day services and community involvement. Without his work we would not be in the position we are today, and we hope that he would have appreciated the progress we have made.

We are very grateful to SCIE for funding the knowledge review, and to Bernie Ward for her support and encouragement along the way. Sincere thanks are also owed to Marie Broad at FPLD who so efficiently organised the workshops, and to Sammantha Cave at Norah Fry who was involved in formatting the reports. Members of the Valuing People Support Team and Louise McQuillan of Northern Ireland Mencap were extremely helpful in co-facilitating workshops.

We are grateful for the interest and support shown by everyone who attended workshops, especially the self-advocates and family members. People were very keen that community-based opportunities and services grow and develop, and represent a fantastic force for change. We'd also like to thank all those who took time to answer questions, both in telephone interviews and on visits. The visits were arranged at fairly short notice and managers, staff, people with learning disabilities and family members willingly gave their time and energy to help. Their open, frank discussions were very revealing and thought-provoking. We hope that the review reports do justice to the information people have contributed.

Finally, a big thank you to the members of the two teams that undertook visits to services: Mouse England and Robert Butler (self-advocates), Rachel Mason and Elaine French (parents), Ann Lloyd and Paul St Quintin (commissioners). The teams performed a very demanding job in an energetic and insightful way, and contributed enormously to the review.

Executive summary

Introduction

This knowledge review brings together key themes and issues emerging from a review of the UK literature and a survey of best practice.[*] The work was commissioned by SCIE (Social Care Institute for Excellence) and was undertaken by the Foundation for People with Learning Disabilities (FPLD) and Norah Fry Research Centre (NFRC) working in partnership.

The knowledge review addresses a specific question:

> What has, and what has not contributed to the successful provision of community-based day activities for all people with learning disabilities?

'Successful provision' of community-based day activities was taken to imply that people would be 'having a good day'. National policy[43] indicates that 'a good day' is about people with learning disabilities:

- undertaking activities that have a purpose
- being in ordinary places, doing things that most members of the community would be doing
- doing things that are right for them personally
- receiving support that meets their individual and specific requirements and overcomes inequalities
- meeting local people, developing friendships, connections and a sense of belonging.

Developing successful community-based day activities

Overview

As recently as 2005, a national survey of people with learning disabilities found that 39 per cent of all people with a learning disability were attending a day centre, of whom two-fifths were attending five days a week.[3].

It also found that one in six had a paid job compared with two-thirds of men and half of women in the general working age population. Two thirds of the people who were unemployed and able to work said they wanted a job, but the range of jobs likely to be attained is narrow, with a pattern of low hours and low wages. Mencap has estimated that 20,000 people have *no* form of support or provision at all for structured activities outside the home during the day (Mencap 2002 a,[21]).

It is evident that many local authorities are still struggling to move away from large, congregate settings, and to achieve increased provision to meet demand. The most progressive of new initiatives are changing and developing as they face the realities of implementing new models and approaches. It is also clear that development is 'situational', affected by the local social, political, economic and demographic context. It is a varied and evolving picture around the UK.

There is a dearth of good quality evaluative research on the impact of day services for people with learning disabilities, although employment provision has received more attention. Research inevitably lags behind practice, but in the case of community-based day activities there has been little formal research. The intervening period has seen significant new policy directives across the UK. The practice survey focused on *best* practice so there are dangers in generalising from the findings. The move to more community-based models of support requires structured research to assess the *extent* to which people really are 'having a good day'.

Ingredients for effective change and barriers to achieving it

The research review identifies eight **key ingredients** for achieving successful community-based provision, including employment, learning and leisure. It also highlights a number of barriers. The barriers are echoed in the practice survey, and others have emerged. They are explored here in relation to the eight key ingredients, with a further four or five key ingredients suggested on pages 8 and 9. The main messages from research are presented in italics, followed by findings from practice.

Partnerships with people and their families

People who use services, including families as 'indirect' users, should be central to the process of modernisation.

This can be achieved through their involvement in service design and development, and through person-centred individualised planning. In practice, partnerships are developing through:

- the inclusion of people with learning disabilities and family carers on steering groups, reference groups and on boards of management
- person-centred planning based on circles of support (or planning circles), though as yet this remains small scale.

Self-advocacy groups are leading some innovative and successful projects which increase people's social and leisure opportunities, and provide information about what's going on locally – but partnerships with those organisations are fragile, as evidenced by their insecure, short-term contractual and funding arrangements.

Some parents have had a positive impact by organising direct payments and individualised support for their sons and daughters, and initiating service developments. However, the influence of parents is largely described negatively in terms of blocking planned initiatives, both at service development and individual level: the shape of community-based service developments reflect parental concerns and influence. The message from practice is that partnerships with families need time and a face-to-face approach to develop.

Leadership

Lack of a clear direction and lead is a barrier. Leadership and change agents are needed at local and national level, with consensus about the role and function of day services. People with learning disabilities, family carers, staff, employers and community members can all be leaders.

Leadership is evident in practice through:

- the influence of national policies and support. They have been well-received and there is clarity about the outcomes that services are working to help people achieve
- the action of self-advocacy groups in developing local social opportunities

- the influence of individuals who take 'the wider view', develop net-works, and are committed and determined to achieve community inclusion.

The way that local areas organise to achieve social inclusion and an ordinary life are very variable. They reflect local resources, political priorities and ethos. Power and decision-making about major change does not lie with leaders of local authority learning disability services. This can be a constraint.

Leadership from people with learning disabilities and families is hav-ing some impact, but it remains on the fringes at the moment and much more could be happening. We are not sure if this is about the will to do it, or practicalities around support.

Cultural change in services

People are likely to resist change, and the culture of day centres may persist into community settings. People need exposure to alternatives. Strategic managers need to work to a new paradigm.

There is some evidence that cultural change is being achieved through:

- at least some staff in most services being training in person-centred approaches
- services stressing the need to 'think like a business' to build partner-ships with a wide range of community bodies in order to achieve the opportunities and support that people want
- positive experiences (exposure to alternatives) impacting on the way people with learning disabilities, family carers and staff think
- increased focus on and development of social firms, social enterprises and self-employment.

New-style community-based services are mostly operating from a base, many shared by other community groups or public services. There is a danger that segregated cultures will persist unless services have clear strategies to achieve integrated opportunities and community connec-tions. Those strategies are not very evident as yet.

Development of services targeted specifically at people from black and minority ethnic groups suggests that a culture of more inclusive and ethnically sensitive provision is developing. There are few signs that this is actually the case *beyond* those targeted services (which are not widespread) and person-centred planning or individual funding initiatives.

In general, supported employment services can supply formal evaluations, often led or required by external organisations. There is a culture of evidence-based, outcomes-focused provision. Few other community-based day services have developed that culture as yet. There are tendencies to showcase developments, possibly as a result of having to work hard to persuade politicians, senior managers and family carers to back community-based provision.

Personalised planning with and for people

Person centred planning enhances people's community involvement, contact with friends, contact with family and choice, but seems to have no impact on access to more inclusive social networks, employment, and physical activity. It is best considered as an evolutionary step towards the increasing individualisation of supports and services.

In practice:

- local strategies emphasise person-centred approaches and an 'ordinary life' value-base
- for people who have person-centred plans changes are being achieved, often linked to individualised funding and family involvement
- supported employment schemes are delivering individualised, person-centred planning for work and are achieving results
- more personalised planning is evident in many different forms.

Overall, improvements in what's happening for most individuals are to do with the opportunities that come from being community-based, and services being more generally person-centred in the way they operate. The level of formal person-centred planning in many areas is not high.

Individualised funding and direct payments

To achieve more individualised approaches money needs to be released from centre-based services and be focused on individuals. There is limited evidence about how people are using individualised funding for support with activities outside the home.

Feedback from the 'in-control' pilot sites and people using direct payments suggest that with individualised funding, people reduce their use of organised day services, but the change is in small steps over time.
The practice survey also suggests that:

- most new community-based developments have been achieved with no extra revenue funding
- community care purchasing budgets are under pressure, in part because of increased take-up of direct payments
- money is not being released from the block funding of day services and transferred into purchasing budgets. It is a complex challenge that is not yet being faced.

'Smart' commissioning

There are three key tasks: overseeing the transition from a centre-based to a community-based service; reconfiguring and using resources in specialist and mainstream community services to meet needs, including unmet needs; developing commissioning that responds to the needs of individuals.

Research identifies issues around poor strategic leadership, poor partnerships, lack of emphasis on employment, and shortage of properly trained care managers. In practice:

- some areas have transferred revenue or staff from 'old' day services into employment services to extend capacity, but there are still problems meeting demand for employment support

- some day services are taking an active role in preparing people for work, but overall the role of day services in relation to employment is not clear and does not have a strategic push
- availability of capital money has impacted on developments and has been used mainly for new community bases. Some more accessible changing facilities in community places have been achieved using capital money
- many voluntary sector services do not know if, or how, they link into the local modernisation strategy. Developments are not sufficiently 'joined up' across providers to give a coherent, planned network of opportunities and support to meet needs
- the majority of services can provide information about budgets, but not about how much the service is costing for individuals
- removing the division between residential and day supports can help people to have a more 'whole life' *if and when* person-centred planning underpins support. Service providers with such an approach are relatively rare and may need to be 'grown' in local areas
- information from implementation and outcomes of individualised planning is not yet being used strategically to inform future developments.

Many people have moved from five days a week using a single service to accessing support from a mix of services. People who need high levels of support do *not* have such diverse opportunities and choices, except where they are in receipt of direct payments. The trend appears to be towards small but 'special' bases with tailored equipment and facilities. Few supported employment schemes and social firms are serving people with high support needs. Unequal opportunities persist and it is a major concern.

Staff development

Staff skills and attitudes make a real difference and can add value to a service. Staff need to be targeted to the needs of individuals, and to work in person-centred ways. Doing an activity in a community setting does not equal social inclusion. New job descriptions, real career opportunities and training for staff are required, particularly to develop skills in social inclusion, community mapping and bridge building.

Modernised day services and employment services describe positive and enthusiastic staff. We can see that:

- to varying degrees, modernised services have changed the way they use staff. A range of new roles and responsibilities have developed
- some staff still have 'old' day service job descriptions and contracts, but are working differently through good will and good team management
- it helps when services have a clear 'ordinary life' value-base that permeates all levels and systems
- people with learning disabilities and family carers are delivering training to staff in specialist *and* general community services.

Recruiting and retaining staff is an issue for some services and for some individuals using direct payments. Use of agency staff by some services may be high as a deliberate policy to reduce costs. The impact on quality of service is not clear.

A more strategic approach is needed at practice level to help people achieve community connections and inclusion. Teams of staff, including supported employment teams, need to know and agree what their strategies are, and they need training and support in putting the strategies into practice.

Developing people's independence is an important aim. To achieve it, day service staff need training and support to use structured approaches for skills teaching and fading support.

Community capacity building

A community infrastructure that welcomes people with learning disabilities needs to be built. It's about more than supporting people to be present in the community and requires a strategic approach.

Some strategies appear to be yielding positive results:

- a focus on 'local' support and opportunities for people, reducing reliance on transport and helping people build sustainable relationships and a sense of belonging
- building new partnerships with community and mainstream organisations to create positive new opportunities for people (though many are arising from practice and chance opportunities rather than being strategically-led)
- using 'mobility' benefits to achieve individualised travelling solutions for people.

Of particular concern, though, is the number of new initiatives set up with short-term funding. Some of the most person-centred and inclusive practices were found in small projects and employment schemes with insecure and fragmented funding. Sustainability is an issue.

Use and development of integrated further education opportunities appears extremely rare. Provision of individualised support for people to access college courses is an issue. Research identifies availability of personal support as, generally, a significant barrier to the achievement of person-centred community activities, and this is echoed loudly in practice.

There continue to be major organisational barriers to the development of improved transport for most people, particularly managers not having control over transport budgets.

Other key ingredients for effective change

There are five that are indicated from the practice survey:

- **good information** for people so that they can make choices, including information about the relationship between benefits and work to overcome continuing fears. Disseminating the experience of people with learning disabilities and family carers helps, as do 'tasters', and regular 'what's on' information. Some self-advocacy groups have proven expertise in this area
- **developing support and services that 'divert' people** so they do not begin to use day services, including person-centred transition planning for young people and employment support for people who do

not meet eligibility criteria for local authority services, but who may develop difficulties if unoccupied during the day

- **political will and support**. Without this, community-based support and services will be slow to develop
- **skilled team management** giving day-to-day direction, actively focusing staff time on delivering the results that people with learning disabilities want to achieve, supporting with problem-solving, and systematically monitoring service delivery to ensure quality. With direct payments it may be a person with learning disabilities or a family carer that is 'the manager'
- **wider partnership working**. In areas that demonstrated very good practice in moving towards individualised, community-based solutions, partnership was part of the service culture. Partnership working needs to encompass partnerships between service commissioners and providers, as well as wider community organisations and services. There needs to be more of an emphasis on cooperation and joint planning, and less on competition.

Gaps in knowledge

Significant gaps in information about current practice and in the knowledge base for practice are indicated. They reflect the paucity of research on day services for people with learning disabilities to date and the recent paradigm change that has resulted in new ways of supporting people to 'have a good day'.

Information about current practice

Community-based support for day activities is complex. It covers a wide range of providers and models of delivery, which has implications for research. Sufficient time and resources are needed to explore gaps around:

- the role, function and impact of day activities, including the quality of delivery and outcomes for people
- provision of community-based day opportunities for people from minority ethnic communities, people with profound and multiple

learning difficulties, people who present challenging behaviours, and people in older and younger age categories
- what's happening in further education and lifelong learning services
- the 'clubhouse' model as a way of shifting power and control into the hands of people with learning disabilities
- effective models and strategies for recruiting, training and developing staff into new roles
- the costs of new community-based models of support and services.

Gaps in knowledge underpinning practice

Practice guidance, information and development opportunities are needed:
for commissioners, managers and care managers around:

- costing services
- monitoring of community-based service delivery
- lessons from Learning and Skills Council Pathfinder projects
- effective, person-centred transition planning
- how to release money from the block funding of day services.

for local politicians and board members around:

- policy and best practice in day service modernisation
- funding strategies for sustainability.

for staff in community-based day services around:

- Training in Systematic Instruction
- work preparation, including developing self-employment
- strategies for achieving inclusion and building community connections.

for managers and staff in social firms and sheltered workshops around:

- how to moving on to a business footing
- self-employment (micro-enterprise).

These areas require further research, evaluation, practice guidance or development effort. From our experience during this work, more information and guidance will be welcomed and will help people with learning disabilities to 'have a good day'.

Introduction

This report is the final product of a knowledge review – comprising a research review and a practice survey – which set out to identify 'what has, and what has not contributed to successful provision of community-based day activities for people with learning disabilities' (SCIE 2005). The review was carried out for SCIE by a team from the Foundation for People with Learning Disabilities (FPLD) and Norah Fry Research Centre (NFRC).

The 'Having a Good Day' review was about services and support for people with learning disabilities to do the things they want to do 'during the day', including at weekends and in the evenings. The study was about what people are being supported to do in ***ordinary community places***. In the past 20 years there has been a significant paradigm shift, from people having a 'day service' and going to a day centre, to services supporting people in:

- workplaces
- education classes and colleges
- sports and leisure centres
- local community centres
- and around local villages and towns.

In essence, the Having a Good Day study was about how to develop and organise opportunities, support and services so that people can take up ordinary opportunities and have ordinary lifestyles. The study was about how things have changed:

- what services *are doing* to help people to 'have a good day' using ordinary community places
- what services *are finding hard*, and the *support they need*.

The study looked at 'modernised services' as well as totally new initiatives. It looked at what is happening for **all** people with learning disabilities, including people from black and minority ethnic communities, people with complex needs, and people whose behaviour is challenging.

Having a good day

The work was all about what needs to happen so that people 'have a good day'.

Having a good day is about:

- doing things that have a purpose
- being in ordinary places, doing things that most members of the community would be doing
- doing things that are right for you
- receiving support that meets your needs
- being in touch with local people, meeting people and developing friendships.

Research review

2.1 Introduction

This research review is about community-based day activities for people with learning disabilities. It draws out key themes and issues from the UK literature on this topic. This review is one part of a wider project called 'Having a Good Day?', commissioned by the Social Care Institute for Excellence (SCIE) from the Foundation for People with Learning Disabilities (FPLD) and the Norah Fry Research Centre (NFRC), University of Bristol.

The purpose of the review was to systematically identify and evaluate research evidence about the provision of community-based day activities and opportunities for all people with learning disabilities. In doing so, we have:

1. Analysed previous published knowledge on the modernisation of day activities.
2. Taken account of issues of diversity and diverse contexts, including rural areas.
3. Reviewed the way partnership boards and person-centred planning strategies have impacted on the development of community-based day activities.
4. Identified gaps in the available knowledge and literature.
5. Highlighted areas that would benefit from practice guidance.

We took community-based day activities and employment support to be those provided by both specialist and mainstream statutory services (including social services, further and continuing education and local authority leisure services) and independent or voluntary organisations. We included literature about community-based activities supported by staff from day centres, but excluded any activities that took place wholly in day centres. We also included further education college courses, adult education classes, and activities supported by staff from supported living or residential care services. The activities described in this review all take place outside the person's own home, although it must be recognised that some practitioners and policy makers are now thinking more holistically about support for an individual. Literature about activities relating to work, jobs and volunteering was also included where people received support either to undertake those activities (for example, through supported employment and volunteering services), or to organise them (for example, through social firms and social enterprises). Some social firms and enterprises were excluded because they were based wholly in day centres. Literature about the experiences of people in independent (unsupported) employment was not included in the review on the grounds that it described people who were not receiving a service.

A technical appendix to the review provides a detailed account of how the review was carried out. In summary, the review covered UK research reported in academic articles, formal and informal accounts of practice, unpublished pieces of work, and the 'grey' literature on day opportunities for people with learning disabilities published since 1997.

The review is written in five sections. The first presents an overview of community-based day opportunities. The second addresses the process of change and modernisation that has taken place in day services over the past eight years, commencing with the publication of two influential documents – *Moving into the mainstream* and the *Changing days* report. The third section focuses on the most intensively researched day activities (work, jobs and employment) and the fourth on education and leisure opportunities. The final section concerns outcomes in day activities, including those areas that appear not to be represented in the literature.

2.2 Community-based day opportunities: an overview

Since the late 1980s a wide range of community-based alternatives to 'traditional' day services have emerged in the UK. These include a range of employment-related support, access to adult and continuing education, use of leisure and recreational services, befriending schemes and other forms of more generic 'without walls' provision that operate outside of day centres. Simons and Watson[1] summarise these different forms of community-based day opportunities as follows:

- Initiatives that focus on **performing arts** – these tend to be locally based, with a limited life and often aim to promote 'citizenship' for people with learning disabilities.*
- Initiatives that are concerned with **places** – these use community facilities such as leisure centres, shops, cinemas, sports, etc and operate as outreach activities from a local base. They provide people with opportunities for community presence and inclusion.
- Initiatives that focus on **relationships** – these aim to help people with learning disabilities to develop friendships and relationships in the wider community through befriending schemes, 'leisure link' schemes and workplaces.
- Initiatives that attempt to build a comprehensive strategy for **opening up a wide range of opportunities**, such as those emanating from the Changing Days Project.**

The literature about these developments indicates that they are very often heavily reliant on individual initiatives and the interests of particular staff.[2] Historically, it also appears that the day centre has continued to dominate in terms of scale of provision,[1] despite policy exhortations to the contrary. As late as 2005, 39% of all adults with a learning disability

---

* Some projects, such as the Elfrida Society's Democratic Participation Project, are directly concerned with engaging people with learning disabilities in the political process. See *Community Living* (2002) vol 16, no 2, pp 20-21.

** The Changing Days Project (1994-97) worked with five development sites to promote and support the implementation of community-based daytime opportunities. Central to the project's objectives was the premise that services should be centred on individual needs and community inclusion, not containment and segregation.

were attending a day centre, two-fifths of whom were attending five days a week.[3*]

2.2.1 The rationale for community-based day opportunities

There is great agreement about the potentially deleterious effects of segregated support and the desirability of locating future support in community settings. One of the alleged consequences of spending years of their lives in day centres is that people have low expectations of what can be achieved in their lives because they rely on a narrow range of people for support.[4–6] Indeed, day services have usually been provided in segregated settings,[1] affording the people who use them few opportunities to develop links with non-disabled members of their local community or access generic education, sport or leisure facilities,[7] although *Fulfilling lives* noted that some large and seemingly 'traditional' day centres in fact offer a range of outreach and community-based services.[8]

This does not mean that people are necessarily dissatisfied with the day services they use, although there are very few large-scale studies exploring this issue. Emerson et al's[3] survey reported that nearly everyone (96 per cent) who went to a day centre said they liked going and only a quarter said they would like to change what they did in the daytime. Simons and Watson[1] found that those using day centres tended to be positive about them, while those who had moved onto other day activities, such as employment or further education, tended to be negative about

---

[*] The survey from which these figures were drawn also found that some people were more likely to go to a day centre than others: if they had higher support needs, were older, were not poor, lived in residential care or a Supporting People scheme, were women, lived in a less deprived area, or were Asian. This survey, of 2,898 people with learning disabilities, aimed to establish from people with learning difficulties themselves what their whole lives were like including where they lived and with whom, what they did during the day, and what their needs, wants and aspirations were. It also sought to describe current use of services, views on the services, to help establish what the gaps were between what is currently provided for people with learning difficulties and what they would like.

day centres. These findings were echoed by Ward[2] who reported many people were bored attending a day centre and expressed greater interest in activities run outside a day centre setting, and Jahoda and Markova[9] who found that people moving from home and from long-stay hospital to living arrangements in the community believed attendance at a day centre to be stigmatising. Questionnaire returns from more than 1,000 people with learning disabilities canvassed for their views about the arts showed that almost 90 per cent preferred integrated or inclusive activities to those arranged within traditional day service settings.[10]

It seems then that exposure to alternatives to traditional day services and the location of daytime support is a factor in people's satisfaction with the day service they receive. Hall[11] argues that this debate is more nuanced than is generally acknowledged. The discrimination, abuse and rejection that they suffer at the hands of the community has led some people with learning disabilities to seek '"safe spaces" and networks. Where new forms of "normality" and inclusions can be shaped'[11, p 304]. Thus some activities that take place in community settings are purposely segregated, such as theatre companies and nightclubs that '"honour" learning disabled people's entertainment'[12, p 827*], performance arts designed to explore the experience of having a learning disability,[13] using services,[14] or to nurture people's ability to manage and run their own activities. A community development project run by The Elfrida Society, for example, supported and mentored people with learning disabilities to establish sustainable community groups, some of which became com-

---

* Several magazine articles describe the rationale for segregated clubs: *Community Living* (2002) vol 16, no 1, pp 14–15, *Community Living* (2002) vol 16, no 2, pp 14–15, *Community Living* (2004) vol 18, no 2, pp 14–15.

munity enterprises, controlled and run by themselves. These included a football club,* a nightclub, a credit union and a training service.[15]**

Some take the debate about self-segregation in day opportunities further. According to Cummins and Lau,[16] policy and research on social integration pays too much attention to achieving and measuring physical integration and not enough to facilitating 'connectedness' within communities of people with learning disabilities. They point to the potentially negative effects of exposing people with severe disabilities to stressful environments such as schools and workplaces and suggest that it is only 'ideological prejudice' that prevents practitioners and policy makers from encouraging 'self-perceived social connectedness' among this group based on their disability. It should be mentioned here that self-advocacy activities, for instance within People First groups, are based on the model of peer support, and often provide very meaningful and valued day opportunities.[17] Yet a small-scale experiment in fostering personal relationships among a group of people with severe learning disabilities had limited success because it relied on staff sustaining the group and any benefits to the group members were unclear.[18]

Satisfaction may also be determined by what people do when they are being supported to undertake day activities. Respondents to the recent national survey[3] described a range of activities undertaken during the previous month. Almost all had been shopping, most had visited friends and family, had been to a restaurant, pub, cafe or club, or been to a hairdresser. Substantial numbers had played sport or gone swimming, seen a film at a cinema, a play or a concert, visited a library, or watched a sporting event. Small numbers had done all or all but one of

---

** Gary Wilkinson, manager of Arsenal Ladies football team, said 'it is good that we as people with learning difficulties have built up a team – that shows we can do things ourselves' (*Community Living*, January/February 2000, p 7).

** Some of the arts projects sponsored by The Elfrida Society have struggled to find mainstream facilities: see *Community Living* (2002) vol 16, no 2, pp 12–13. Elsewhere day services have forged alliances with professional artists, leading to performances by people with learning disabilities in mainstream venues (see 'Art for people's sake', *Community Care*, June 8, 2000).

these activities and only 5 per cent had done none or only one of them. The findings reveal that people with a learning disability are at least as likely to participate in some types of community-based activities, such as going to the cinema, attending a concert and watching sport, as the general population. Asked what they would like to do more of during the daytime, their priorities were to go out, get a job (or a different job), sports, visit people and generally have more things to do. Others mentioned having money for things, moving on from college/day centre, going shopping, using a computer, going out to pub/meals, going to a day centre more often, listening to music and doing arts and crafts.[3]

The largest longitudinal study of the resettlement of people with learning disabilities from hospital also contained powerful messages about people's priorities in daytime activities. Structured interviews with almost two hundred people revealed that they preferred activities that are not associated with day centres: outings, education and work, relaxation and leisure.[19] This confirmed earlier findings suggesting that a proportion of those using day centres would prefer an alternative – such as paid work, voluntary work, college – although some wanted to take up these options and 'keep a foot in the door' of the day centre.[1]

This sense of 'keeping a foot in the door' is important since most activities outside centres do not equate to full-time provision.[20] Mencap's review of day services concluded that while the best run community or home-run services are user-led, with people deciding for themselves what they wish to do and how they can best develop their own skills, these types of services rarely offer a five-day a week service.[21]

Doing an activity in a community setting does not automatically ensure that an individual has contact with non-disabled people or is living 'an ordinary life'.[21] Baker found that compared to a staff control group, a small sample of people with learning disabilities took part in fewer activities, less frequently and were more likely to do so with staff or carers than on their own or with friends.[22] Srivastrava's study of 26 people moving from a long-stay hospital concluded that 'both leisure and friendship are areas of life which can lead to integration in the community for a person, and they are closely related'[23, p 23], while improved access to leisure can also lead to improved physical well being and the development of choice by people using these services.[24] Forrester-Jones concurs, but suggests that 'leisure cannot be the mainstay of a person's life' [25, p 30] and needs to be complemented by other activities, such as employment, that also promote social networks.

Other factors may influence people's experience of doing activities in the community. A study of quality in residential and day services for a sample of 56 people with learning disabilities in England found that frequency of community integration, extent of autonomy and level of activity were associated with the ability of the individuals.[26] Abraham et al[27] found that age determined the nature of the association between community participation and self-esteem among users of day services. A possible explanation for this is 'that age alters the experience of community participation so that it enhances self-esteem among older people with learning difficulties but challenges self-esteem amongst younger people with learning difficulties'. [27, p 442]

2.2.2 Barriers to the development of community-based day opportunities

The Changing Days Project identified a number of structural factors that can hinder the development of community-based day opportunities for people: a lack of emphasis on employment; poor partnerships between agencies; a shortage of properly trained care managers; and inadequate healthcare for people with learning disabilities.[28] The inability of traditional services to respond flexibly to individual needs and wishes has been ameliorated in some areas by the availability of direct payments. Pearson,[29] for example, cites the case of Paul who stopped attending a local day centre because he had become fed up with the activities on offer there, but found a solution by employing a personal assistant, using a direct payment, to do the things he really wanted to do during the daytime. Simone Aspis,[30] a member of People First, argues that services should worry less about providing a menu of options and concentrate more on listening to what people say they want and meeting those needs through direct payments.

There is substantial research evidence about benefits being a major barrier to people with learning disabilities getting a job,[31] while National Minimum Wage legislation has also had implications for the practice of offering people 'voluntary work' and payment in kind.[32] A survey of employment agencies found that following the introduction of the national minimum wage, average hourly rates of pay for people with learning disabilities increased, although average weekly rates of pay did not. As people with learning disability are far more likely to be in supported employment than other care groups, the explanation seems to be that adjustments were made to their paid and unpaid hours to protect their entitlement to benefits.[33] Further data from Delphi groups of employers of disabled people and disability employment advisors confirmed that while the National Minimum Wage has improved pay rates for disabled people in work, there have been negative implications for some employers' perceptions of the associated costs and complications about benefit entitlement.[34]

Some writers have identified a lack of adequate social skills training as an inhibitor to social integration for people with a learning disability,[35] inappropriate methods for helping people to make choices, and a thin evidence base on choice to guide practitioners.[36] The managers of residential homes in two English cities cited the unavailability of transport, inadequate financing and the lack of staffing to provide one-to-one support as reasons why greater use could not be made of community facilities for 'creative leisure' activities such as listening to music, art, playing music, dance, needlecraft and drama.[37] The users of a range of services in one metropolitan borough also highlighted transport and lack of personal support as barriers to accessing non-segregated services.[38]

2.2.3   Outcomes in day services

The literature describing the evolution from segregated to community-based daytime support for people with learning disabilities rarely addresses the question of what such services are designed to achieve. Felce et al[26] suggest that a consensus about the role and function of day services has not been reached, while another study concluded that day services are all too often 'aimless' and 'ill-defined', offering little more than an alternative to being at home.[21] Key questions that still need to be posed, besides the function and purpose of day services, include the extent and scope of current provision and the degree of shortfall.[2]

The lack of consensus about what day services are intended to achieve has, according to some, contributed to a dearth of evaluative research on the impact of day services. In their own Research Review, Simons and Watson[1] grouped evidence from the very small amount of material that pertains to outcomes in day services into four categories. These indicate the broad domains that outcome measures might attempt to illuminate:

- engagement in meaningful activities
- time spent in a non-segregated setting
- extending people's social networks
- generating income for people (including wages, benefits, charges).

Despite a lack of research in this area, by far the most detailed tool for measuring outcomes and impact of community-based day services is the Day Services Modernisation toolkit, [39] which has been designed to help Learning Disability Partnership Boards write their day service modernisation plans. The toolkit has two parts: the first includes a vision of a modernised day service, an audit tool and some key contacts. The second includes more detailed information on implementing strategies for modernisation of day services.

2.3 Achieving change: modernising day services

2.3.1 Policy and legislative background

The modernisation of day services has been on the policy agenda since the late 1990s. *Moving into the mainstream*[40] (Department of Health, 1998) urged local authorities to diversify the range of residential and day services available to the people in need of support. It predicted that the transition from older, industrial employment ATC (adult training centre) models to resource and recreational models was not without problems and the rate of change could be slow, not least because some users' parents sought to maintain 'the security of large centres providing five day-a-week care exclusively on the centre premises'. [40, p 19]

A year later, *Facing the facts*[31] again highlighted the dominance of large ATCs and social education centres (SECs) in day care provision. A survey of 24 local authorities and their partner health organisation found these institutions accounted for 66 per cent of provision, compared to 16 per cent of day placements supplied by continuing education, 9 per cent through outreach groups, 7 per cent through supported employment, and 2 per cent in NHS managed day services.[*] The survey also found considerable variations between authorities as to the amount and type of day provision available, and noted concerns about reductions in service levels and loss of structured routines as day services began to reconfigure.[31]

Meanwhile, *The same as you?*,[41] a review of services for people with learning disabilities living in Scotland, rehearsed many of the arguments about the state of day services provision south of the border, noting that there were 'people going to day centres for many years without a formal assessment' [41, p 54] and that users and carers described services as boring and lacking in direction. The Scottish review presented a more cautious assessment of the need to access generic adult education and supported employment services, with an acknowledgement that 'there is still a place for sheltered workshops'. [41, p 60]. In Wales, *Fulfilling the promises*[42] found evidence of some variety in day provision (more community placement options, further education, work experience) and less reliance on large day centres, but problems in developing supported employment due to difficulties with the benefits system. It also noted a trend towards sessional attendance rather than people spending their whole week in a single setting.

Valuing People[43, p 19] provided the first English national strategy for day services, an area of public service provision that was described as 'frequently failing to provide sufficiently flexible and individual support'. The White Paper therefore set a new objective for day services, that of enabling 'people with learning disabilities to lead full and purposeful lives within their community and to develop a range of friendships, activities and relationships'. [43, p 76] While recognising the role that day centres had traditionally played in providing respite care to families, the White Paper set out a five-year programme for localities to improve day opportunities. Learning and Skills Councils (LSCs) were to ensure people with a learning disability had equality of access to education, action was to be taken to outlaw discrimination against them on public transport, and councils' leisure plans were to address their needs.

The centrepiece of the five-year programme was an obligation placed on each partnership board to write a day service modernisation plan by

---

[*] Figures quoted refer to the percentage of whole-time equivalent day places available.

February 2003. The infrastructure to support modernisation included a nationally produced 'toolkit', advice and guidance from regional advisors on the Valuing People Support Team and financial assistance in the form of the Learning Disabilities Development Fund (LDDF).

Concern had already been expressed about ensuring a consistency of approach and avoiding duplication of effort from area to area in any national plan. Simons and Watson[1] suggested developing a regional 'model service' framework that could be used to disseminate and share good practice and ensure a strategic approach to the development of day services. In 2003 the Valuing People Support Team conducted regional reviews of plans to modernise day services. Although we were only able to access four of the nine potential reports, some fairly consistent themes emerged. Strategy development and practical action was underway in all areas but some local authorities were more advanced than others. A small number of authorities had set targets for access to basics such as person-centred planning, direct payments and paid employment. But equally, plans from many areas showed evidence of lack of action, or poor understanding about what these key components of modernisation involved. Staff development continued to be an issue, particularly in terms of provision of training for developing skills in social inclusion, community 'mapping' and bridge building. Similarly, the issue of transport remained problematic, with local authorities citing the barriers of inflexibility and high costs of specialised transport and a lack of accessibility of public transport.

These findings largely concur with those expressed in the inspection report *Fulfilling lives*[8] which, in the wake of *Valuing People*, highlighted the slow pace of change and lack of partnership approaches to the provision of services for people with learning disabilities. In relation to day services, the need for a programme of modernisation to promote social inclusion was emphasised.

2.3.2 Principles for good practice in designing support for day opportunities

Simons and Watson,[1] drawing on research by Felce et al[26] and McIntosh and Whittaker,[44] proposed a 'service design for an ordinary community life' comprising three principles:

1 **An ordinary context:** real activities should take place in real settings with natural supports from co-participants in an activity. Dowson[20] adds that although the development of relationships with community members in non-segregated mainstream settings should be a guiding principle for services, they should also acknowledge that some people with learning disabilities may want to spend time with others who have similar life experiences. A full and flexible service would support activities through the working week, in the evenings and at weekends.[21]

2 **Organisation:** clear outcomes should be identified relating to participation, independence, relationships and choice. Staffing should be determined by need and the availability of 'natural supports', including advocates, where appropriate, and people other then those employed to provide support.[21] Paid support staff and natural supporters will require training for their respective roles. A range of working methods should be identified, such as individual planning. Dowson[20] and Mencap[21] also call for enough support to each person to ensure that carers are able to pursue their own careers/interests.

3 **Quality:** activities should suit individual interests and concerns. Such activities should enable people to develop their skills and potential[21] with a special emphasis given to the achievement of paid employment[20]. The quality of support (in doing any activity, in establishing relationships, and in getting to and from activities) should be appraised.

So what are the necessary, if not sufficient, ingredients for modernising day services using these guiding principles? From the literature we have distilled out eight key conditions for change:

- partnership with people and their families
- leadership
- cultural change in services
- person-centred planning with and for people
- individualised funding and direct payments
- 'smart' commissioning
- Staff development
- community capacity building.

Partnership with people and their families

People who use services should be central to the process of modernisation.[21] Presenting the views of service users directly to senior managers is a persuasive and effective tool for change.[4,44]

Families are also important partners in change since more than half of all adults with a learning disability, including some of those with the highest support needs, live with their families,[3,43] while another 12 per cent live with other relatives.[43] Family carers play a role in supporting people into employment by resolving benefits issues and helping with transport; most value the benefits that work brings to their relative[7] and parents are increasingly leading person-centred planning for their son or daughter.[45–46]

Families are service users in their own right. Implicitly, day services provide a degree of respite for family carers, allowing (crucially for many families) them to pursue paid employment, but the needs, rights and entitlements of carers have rarely been taken into account when designing day services.[1,20] The Changing Days team urged the creation of partnerships with families at the earliest stage of modernisation, utilising their stories to influence the direction of change.[44]

Fulfilling lives concluded that 'more has to be done to win the hearts and minds of carers, who often believe, sometimes with justification, that re-providing a service on a smaller scale can mean reducing the service'.[8, p 35]

Leadership

There will also be a need for leadership and change agents at local and national level.[20] Key to this is the appointment of a senior manager to oversee the modernisation process who is in a position to ensure commitment to the change process from senior managers, elected members and/or board members.[21] Families can and should be involved as change leaders as they can influence other families in ways that managers and paid staff cannot.[4] Evidence from the Changing Days Project also suggests that it is essential to set up a change group to steer the way forward and to involve users, community members, employers, staff and carers in this group.[44, 88]

Changing the culture in services

Dowson[20] exhorts those charged with modernising day services to learn from the experiences of closing hospitals and to pay attention to that fact that the management, staff and users of day centres are likely to resist change just as those associated with long-stay hospitals did. He suggests that the 'inappropriate' culture of day centres may persist beyond the closure of day centre buildings in that staff are liable to over-estimate the value of their own service and under-estimate the capacity of people with learning disabilities to make a success of new opportunities. To counter this the Changing Days team suggested a structured process of change, involving raising awareness of what is good about existing services, what needs to change and learning from examples of good practice elsewhere.[44] Strategic managers also need to re-conceptualise day services as a new paradigm and to 'think themselves' into a new approach beyond conventional financial modelling.[44]

Person-centred planning for and with individuals

A recent report on the experience of using public services found that many disabled people 'felt that they were often trapped in a '"serviceland",' where they had to deal with services that were not structured or delivered in a way that reflected their day to day lives'.[47, para 6.11] Person-centred planning, now acknowledged as an important tool to enable people with learning disabilities to develop meaningful lives[48] is widely promulgated in the modernisation literature. For McIntosh[4] person-centred planning can help young people plan for the ordinary patterns of adult life, rather than getting caught up in traditional segregated services, while the collective picture of the plans has the potential to provide an indicator of priorities in the allocation of resources. In Hackney, for example, a major service redesign was based on the needs and wishes expressed through individual plans based on person-centred approaches, supported by the Changing Days project.[28] In Cardiff 'planning circles' focused on how people wished to spend their time and were facilitated by people selected for their creative thinking skills and commitment to the values espoused by Changing Days.[49]

A recent evaluation of the impact of person-centred planning on the life experience of almost 100 people suggests this emphasis is not misplaced. The research, the 'largest most comprehensive evaluation of the costs and impact of person-centred planning to be undertaken anywhere in the world'[50] concluded that person-centred planning does enhance people's community involvement, contact with friends, contact with family and choice. Successful outcomes were linked to a number of significant factors associated with the process of person-centred planning: the commitment of facilitators, the personal involvement of the focus person and the identity and role of facilitators.

However, person-centred planning appeared to have no impact on access to more inclusive social networks, employment, physical activity and medication. And apparently negative outcomes for people's health simply reflected the fact that for some the project presented the first opportunity for health status to be assessed properly. In summary, the researchers argue that person-centred planning may be best considered as an evolutionary step towards the increasing individualisation of supports and services, not a radical departure with previous practice.[50]

Individualised funding and direct payments

'New style day services require radical new thinking about financial systems, costing and allocating resources'[44, p 153] to release the large sums of money committed to centre-based services. The theory is that all money currently invested in health and local authority services, combined with resources from benefits, wages, education, housing, leisure, etc should be deployed to create and support individual lifestyles for people.[44] The Community Care (Direct Payments) Act 1996 gave disabled people the legal right to receive payment of community care monies and to purchase their own care based on an agreed needs-led assessment.

The Department of Health's community care statistics[48] indicate an 80 per cent rise in the number of adults receiving direct payments during 2003/04 compared with the previous year, although the numbers of direct payment recipients as a proportion of people receiving community care services remains comparatively low.[*] Some groups, including people with learning disabilities, are much less likely to receive direct

---

[*] The *Community care statistics: Referrals, assesssments and packages of care (RAP), England* show that 17,300 adults aged 18 and over received direct payments during 2003, increasing from 9,600 in 2002–03.

payments,[89], although *The story so far* notes a sevenfold increase in the number of people with learning disabilities receiving a direct payment over the past three years, and a doubling of the numbers in last year, a faster rate of increase than that for any other group.[48] Emerson et al's[3] survey suggests that as many as one in five people with a learning disability (19 per cent) now receive a direct payment.

As yet there is limited research evidence about how people with a learning disability are using direct payments although a Scottish pilot project has demonstrated how people with learning disabilities can use direct payments as an alternative to traditional day care.[29] Direct payments provide a way for funding to be tailored to meet people's individual needs by employing their own support workers.[4] Flynn's work revealed that the tasks and qualities required of personal assistants by direct payments recipients and their families[*] ranged from personal care and domestic tasks, sharing activities and pastimes, to knowledge about the supported person's life, empathy, sympathy and trustworthiness.[51]

Research has shown that direct payments can help people to gain confidence, develop new skills and access more individualised packages of support.[52] High levels of satisfaction have been reported among direct payment recipients compared to those using conventional services[53] related to the opportunity to exercise greater choice and control over their support[89, 54] and benefits to their quality of health and social life.[55]

The In-control Project[**] has been piloting the development of self-directed services and individualised funding at a number of sites in the UK and has led to a wider roll-out of 13 individual budget pilot schemes bringing together six different income streams from the Department of Health, the Department for Work and Pensions and the Office of the Deputy Prime Minister, including the Supporting People, Access to Work and Independent Living Programmes. Transport is to be added to this list.

---

[*] Flynn's sample of 16 people included six people with learning disabilities.

[**] More information can be found at www.in-control.org.uk

'Smart' commissioning

The literature identifies three key tasks for commissioners in modernising day services. The first is to oversee the transition from a traditional, centre-based service to a modernised community-based one. Dowson[20] argues that the development of good alternatives to day centres requires a shift from capital to revenue funding, while Mencap advocates protection for existing services, through bridging funds if new services are to be developed before the existing ones are dismantled.[21]

The second task is the reconfiguration of resources available to support day opportunities. This might include mapping current provision and need, setting targets to increase opportunities for people who currently have no access,* ensuring quality, and developing joint working arrangements with providers of generic mainstream services.[21] Simons and Watson[1] talk about 'levering-in' resources by working with leisure, education, employment, housing and regeneration so these services are more responsive to the needs of people with learning disabilities, and drawing on a range of informal supports. They also suggest removing the false distinction in commissioning separate day and residential services. The Changing Days team believed that while significant service change, including a major commitment to supported employment could not be achieved without extra funding, not all change required large inputs of cash. Significant change could be achieved by disaggregating day centre funding, by transfer of staff roles and funding to community-based activities and by more use of direct payments.[28]

The third task looks to future commissioning practices that are attuned to the needs of individual service users. Wilson et al[56] found that the commissioning of day services in a rural area of Scotland were inflexible, dominated by block contracting and devoid of mechanisms by which users and carers could influence what services were purchased. The Changing Days team placed great emphasis on commissioners using outcome data from person-centred plans to draft a new framework for

---

* Mencap believed funds for modernisation allocated by the government were inadequate, arguing for an extra allocation of £120 million per year to the LDDF, plus £140 million to expand day services to 20,000 people who currently have no form of provision.[21]

future services by shifting resources to flexible individual support for users, preferably through direct payments.[44] *Shaping the future together*[95] models how commissioners and strategic planners can use person-centred planning in this way, and emerged from work at two development sites.

Staff development

There is evidence that it is staff skills and attitudes that add value to a service, rather than the building or the number of people attending.[21] Existing resources will need to be used in very different ways, and in particular support from staff will have to be individualised and targeted at the needs of each individual.[1] Staff working in day centres often have no formal training or qualifications and are often casual or temporary staff[21] and staff supporting people in community-based settings will need help to work in person-centred ways through training, new job descriptions [4, 44, 28] and 'real' career opportunities.[21]

Devas[57] distinguishes between the roles of support workers and access workers when people with a learning disability use sports and leisure facilities. Access workers, employed by sports and leisure providers, use disability theory as a foundation of their practice by, for example, working out how activities can be adapted to provide an entry point for a person with a disability. However, the role of the access worker ends at the door to the leisure centre. Support workers know more about the person they are supporting and are charged with helping people try activities in a range of locations, but they may be seen as a buffer between the person they are supporting and the community.

Community capacity building

Bates and Davies[58] talk about the 'social capital' required for true social inclusion, and highlight six components: participation in the local community, reciprocity (looking after one another), feelings of trust and safety, social connections, citizen power and community perception (feeling of belonging).

However, this will not happen simply through community presence since there is little evidence of people being supported to develop wider relationships within their communities.[1]

It is suggested that good social support not only increases community participation, but people are more likely to undertake activities on their own, and less likely to undertake group or supervised activities, if they are able to choose their own support.[27] People with learning disabilities are much less likely to see friends than the general population: in Emerson et al's[3] survey almost a third (31 per cent) said they did not have any contact with friends, and more than two-thirds (69 per cent) had friends who also had a learning disability. One in 20 people (5 per cent) had no friends and did not see anyone from their family. Hospital decommissioning may have resulted in people being physically integrated into local communities, but the social contexts that enabled people to develop long-term friendships have not been replicated.

The Choice Initiative, a programme of development projects focusing on people's need for friendship, concluded that because the sorts of relationships fostered by the projects 'can bring about radical changes in people's lives', services should take them more seriously.[90] Other studies agree that service providers have not supported the development of friendship and social networking.[23, 25] Those charged with supporting people in day activities therefore need to be proactive in building an infrastructure in the community that is welcoming to people,[2] for example, by influencing the design and planning of new buildings such as leisure centres so they are more accessible.[28]

The *Changing days* report highlights the importance of investing in strategies for community inclusion if the modernisation of day services is to succeed. The report enumerates key factors in this process. At the top there should be a commitment from commissioners and providers to make community inclusion a priority, not just a fringe activity, through secure, continuous funding. In organising services there should be a rejection of segregated group activities and an understanding that inclusion means partnership with ordinary citizens. Staff should be recruited who have good connections with their community, bolstered by non-bureaucratic volunteer recruitment. In working with individuals, building social networks should be regarded as an integral part of person-centred planning supported by sensible but flexible risk policies.[44]

Access is a key issue in community capacity building, especially relating to transport. 'Gaining access to private and public transport is central to increasing people's choices, making their lifestyle more varied and improving the overall quality of their lives'.[44, p 175] Transport costs can account for a substantial part of a day services budget and may involve poor service characterised by long journeys and inefficiency, where people are bussed to a day centre first rather than directly to a community-based activity.[21]

Plans for modernisation of day services should give priority to flexible provision of transport, which should include: giving everyone travel training; considering transport requirements in people's individual plans; using direct payments; redesigning public transport and information about transport to make it more accessible; and recognising that special transport can segregate and stigmatise people. Good practice might therefore include vehicles being bought for use by individuals and their supporters, flexibility so that someone can start their journey from home rather than have to go to the day centre first, and use of existing community transport options.[44]

2.4 Work, jobs and employment

A consistent theme throughout the research literature consulted for this review relates to the important, and central, role that employment for people with learning disabilities can play in underpinning the development of community-based day activities. Work is one of the major defining roles in our lives and provides structure to our week as well as generating income.[7, 44] It builds confidence and self-esteem, changing the way people are viewed by family and peers.[44, 59] People with learning disabilities also regard paid work as a way of making a contribution, of being helpful to other people.[7] Yet very few people with learning disabilities are in paid employment of any kind despite work, jobs and employment being given the highest priority in repeated surveys of people's aspirations.[43, 48] According to Dowson,[20] ordinary waged employment is the 'ideal', but is difficult to achieve for most people with a learning disability as repeated studies have revealed the same picture of low levels of employment, low wages and low hours.[60]

The recent national survey[3] provides a detailed statistical picture of the working lives of people with a learning disability, although many of those who responded to the survey did not receive support to undertake their jobs. *Valuing People* estimated that one in ten people with a learning disability were in employment.[*] The national survey put the figure at one in six (17 per cent) people with a learning disability of working age having a paid job, compared to two-thirds of men and half of women in the general working-age population. A small number (6 per cent) said they had an unpaid job, but two-thirds of people with a learning disability who were unemployed and able to work said they wanted a job. Nearly everyone (92 per cent) already in work liked their job, indeed 21 per cent expressed a desire to work longer hours, with just 5 per cent seeking a reduction in the amount of time they were working.

The national survey found that the prospects for these aspirant workers are narrow. They are most likely to find a job (paid or unpaid) in a shop or warehouse, as a gardener or labourer, in catering, in a factory or on an assembly line, in domestic work, as an apprentice or trainee, or as an office worker. They are much more likely than the general population to work part time (less than 16 hours a week) and four-fifths will earn less than £200 per week.

2.4.1 Barriers to work

The benefits system presents a major barrier to people with learning disability seeking work in three ways. Firstly, the models of incapacity central to the benefits system implies that people are incapable for work. Indeed until recently permitted work was termed 'therapeutic work' undertaken following a medical assessment. It also discriminates against people who have never been economically active.[61] Perversely, financial security for many is dependent on them demonstrating their lack of competency (and therefore need for benefits), rather than their competence.[60, 62]

The second barrier to work is well rehearsed, relating to the real or imagined threat to benefits entitlement that taking paid work might entail. For example, most participants in Beyer et al's study[73] worked for less than five hours per week, although a small minority worked more than 16 hours, for fear that benefits would be affected and people would be worse off as a result.

However, the traditional view that benefits are a barrier was challenged by stories of individuals who were financially better off in full-time work and by a growing body of evidence that with the right knowledge and

---

* Recently revised from 10 per cent to 11 per cent.[48]

motivation there are ways to work with the system.[63] Some people place a higher value on their wages than money received from benefits even where the latter option is financially advantageous and work may provide benefits other than wages such as a pension and access to a subsidised canteen.[63] A small but significant number (16 per cent) of those in paid employment in Emerson et al's 2005 survey[3] said they lost some benefits when they started working, but three-quarters of those who lost benefits said this did not cause them any problems, presumably because their pay compensated for the loss of benefits. Ultimately, it may be that the sheer complexity of the benefits system encourages a conservative approach to this problem.[61, 62]

A third way that the benefits system acts as a barrier follows on from the low hours that people generally work in order to protect their entitlements. This could disadvantage people who need more time than is available to learn job skills and may disqualify them from services such as WORKSTEP and Working Tax Credit that are determined by a minimum number of hours worked.[7] Access to Work benefits are no longer dependent on a minimum number of hours worked each week.

Inadequate and inappropriate preparation for work blights the career prospects of many people. Training has been used as a 'displacement' activity, reflected in the lack of relevance of college courses in preparing people for work and sheltered workshops that do not encourage people to move on.[60] This may reflect disabling attitudes held by employers, carers and day services support staff[60] which stems from entrenched service perspectives and the philosophy on which they are based.[62]

Other barriers include difficulties in travel to work and a lack of information about rights to a minimum wage, to join a union, or to time off when sick.[60]

A potentially important route to employment for people with learning disabilities is through programmes funded either by the government (WORKSTEP, Access to work etc) or by local authorities that fund a majority of the estimated 400 supported employment agencies in the UK.[64]

2.4.2 Sheltered employment (WORKSTEP)

Sheltered employment for people with learning disabilities is defined as work with a therapeutic or occupational benefit that is subsidised by non-commercial sources of funding and takes place in a segregated setting. Currently some 7 per cent of adults with learning disabilities of working age are in sheltered employment. The problems associated with this type of provision are a lack of progression to open employment and a limited choice of workshops, thus limiting the choice of trades for people to follow. [60]

2.4.3 Social firms

Social firms grew out of the specific exclusion of people with disabilities from the labour market, it has not always been easy to distinguish from relabelled sheltered workshops. They are, essentially, businesses requiring people with business skills to support them and may not therefore sit easily within a social care framework. However, they can be useful in opening up a wider range of employment opportunities, especially for people with more complex needs for whom very specific environments are required. [1]

---

*   The supported placement scheme is also operated by the WORKSTEP programme and open to people of a certain ability level (30 per cent– 80 per cent as efficient as an ordinary worker). People on the scheme receive the same rates of pay as other workers, but the employer receives a subsidy to cover any difference in performance. Places are limited and this is not a common route into work for people with learning disabilities. [60]

** It is estimated that about 8,500 people with learning disabilities used the WORKSTEP programme in 2001. [64]

*** 'Employment, empowerment and enterprise: report on the values consultation carried out in the social firms sector in 2002', Social Firms UK (www.socialfirms.co.uk/).

**** See, for example, the description of the Burton Street Project in McClimmens. [112]

There are now some 24 social firms solely employing people with a learning disability.[****] The experience of people moving from a traditional day service into a social firm is mixed, with an emphasis on social firms as a good source of a social network rather than achieving career ambitions. Action research with 42 day service users in Luton about vocational alternatives to traditional services found a distinct preference for working in groups through a social firm to achieve the goals of maintaining friendships and engaging in more purposeful activities.[65]

One project in the North West of England transformed four local authority workshops from a therapeutic service into a social enterprise. The aims of the project were to find work experience or jobs in social enterprise for half of these people, to prepare and support people into open employment and to transfer management of the workshops to an independent not-for-profit agency. The project encountered many of the problems previously highlighted in the literature on transforming traditional day services, including the inflexibility of the benefits system and resistance from people's families for them to come off of benefits, the preference of some people for existing arrangements and routines, a fear of losing a place in day services while pursuing open employment, and a lack of appropriate skills and knowledge about the local labour market among day services staff. An evaluation of the project concluded that little substantive change occurred during the period of the project.[66]

A national survey coupled with focus groups resulted in a set of recommendations for good practice in the further development of social firms in the UK. These included greater user participation and empowerment in the development process, the involvement of family carers, expert guidance and welfare rights advice, more opportunities for workers to develop their potential, greater integration of disabled and non-disabled workers and wider consultation with local socioeconomic development agencies.[67]

[*****]Social Firms UK mapping of the sector in 2005 (www.socialfirms.co.uk).

2.4.4 Supported employment and 'real' jobs

Supported employment is based on what Beyer[91] has called the principle of 'place and train', where people with learning difficulties assimilate work-based skills 'on the job', in the workplace. People involved in supported employment have defined successful outcomes for themselves as the development of social skills, acceptance in the workplace, being respected by employers and colleagues, job satisfaction and prospects for moving on.[68] However, there is very little evidence that on their own readiness models help people to progress into open paid employment.[1]

Core funding for supported employment is fragile and fragmented,[60, 62, 64] and provision is patchy, targeted primarily at people with mild or moderate learning disabilities,[69] perhaps indicating that social services departments have not always regarded employment as part of their remit.[1] The Changing Days Programme found that investment in supported employment is still very low and it remains a peripheral service not open to everyone.[4]

The 'perverse incentives' imposed by the UK benefits system appear to be a key factor in explaining why supported employment has not performed in cost-benefit terms as well in the UK as in the US.[1] A pilot study conducted by the Welsh Centre for Learning Disabilities compared the costs and outcomes of supporting a group of seven people with severe learning disabilities and high support needs with a group using a special needs unit in a day centre. While supporting people in employment was more expensive, and the cost-effectiveness of the two support services were similar, the group in supported employment received more assistance and were more engaged in task-related activities. They also experienced greater 'social integration' by virtue of their contact with co-workers and the public.[70] A study of 20 people using a supported employment agency also showed an increase in the size of people's social networks over time.[71] There is some evidence that inclusion in the workplace may be compromised by the presence of specialist job coaches, and some researchers argue that it is better to rely on natural supports, or co-workers.[60]

A recent study by Ridley et al,[63] while noting many factors previously highlighted by research in this field – insecurity of funding; a paucity of full-time jobs; not enough schemes to meet demand; an inequality in access for those with severe disabilities, women and people from minority ethnic communities – also highlighted lack of leadership and an inconsistent framework from which to commission and audit the performance of supported employment. It concluded that supported employment is not firmly embedded as a strategy for improving quality of life and providing opportunities for social inclusion and recommends a more coordinated career-based approach, underpinned by person-centred planning. Self-employment may be the next logical step for some in supported employment as it can offer a better fit with individual values and lifestyle.

Research with 16 people in supported employment in South Wales identified a range of strategies for success in work. These included people training for the disciplines of work, working in different environments and the development of social skills. The research suggested that priorities for employers should be to have open and honest communication with their supported employees, to remove disabling barriers and discriminatory policies and practices, and provide consistent support.[68]

Wilson[72] uses two case studies to illustrate how the pursuit of 'real' or 'normal' jobs, utilising systematic instruction by job coaches, can be disabling because the supported person is unable to complete all of the tasks that a non-disabled employee would be expected to undertake. This can lead to a spiral of despair and falling self-esteem for the person. Reasonable adjustments to working practices to accommodate a person's disability can be an important factor in them getting and retaining a job.

Stevens and Martin[73] cite research by Kemp and Carr[74] to advocate a 'multi-component approach' to supporting people with learning disabilities and 'challenging behaviours' in integrated work settings. Their untested model aspires to marry elements of established supported employment practice with behavioural interventions to increase task competency and productivity for individuals while reducing the likelihood of them exhibiting challenging behaviours in the workplace.

The benefits of work experience were highlighted in a survey of 275 people attending day centres in Belfast that revealed that they were twice as likely to want to get a job if they already had some work experience or if they had pursued some form of further education. The authors conclude that the improvements shown in people's self-esteem, social skills and vocational competence as a result of these experiences make them more likely to succeed in getting and retaining a job.[75]

A recent survey of the outcomes for 200 people using a supported employment service in one English city found staff ratings of service user motivation on entry to the service to be the best predictor of them gaining employment.[76] The researchers tentatively suggest other associations between outcome and services user motivation when leaving the service, their punctuality and the source of their referral to the agency. The scale developed for the research may prove a useful tool in determining the most appropriate pathway for people seeking employment.

2.4.5   Volunteering

Volunteering may be another route to employment or simply meet people's desire to work. A survey of volunteer bureaux by The National Development Team, followed by case study work with six of them, highlighted good practice in providing people with a learning disability with opportunities to be involved in volunteering. The Able Volunteers Programme found that 'focused effort is needed to include volunteers who need additional support. It doesn't just happen'.[77, p 2] With the right support volunteers were able to produce newsletters, serve tea, sell books, distribute food to homeless people, change light bulbs and care for children.

2.4.6   Paid work and housing

Some European countries have linked housing and work in the pursuit of social inclusion for people with learning disabilities by organising access to housing and support through organisations whose primary function is work. This means that most users of such services are able to combine full-time work with a range of housing and support options. In the UK, the link between employment and other life choices for people with learning disabilities has rarely been articulated. This is particularly true for people who live in residential care who are subject to a charging framework that ensures they have no incentive to move off benefits. Work should be an option to everyone regardless of their living arrangements.[61]

2.4.7   Role of day centres in supporting people into work

Day centres vary greatly in the emphasis they place on helping people to find paid work. Beyer et al[7] found that the day centres they visited as part of their study could be grouped as follows:

1. A small group of day services provided little or no employment-related support, with weak links to employment outcomes.
2. The largest group used systems of work skill assessment and formal work preparation, but it was not clear how well these led onto paid jobs.
3. Another group had their own employment placement teams and provided direct support for people with learning disabilities into paid jobs.

Where day centres are focused on employment outcomes they tend to use concepts developed in supported employment (vocational profiling, job matching, job placement, on the job support, career review, etc). Overall there were numerous obstacles to day centres providing an effective employment service in their own right and Beyer et al suggest that appointing work specialists within day centres is not likely to lead to better employment outcomes or to overcome cultural resistance. The study concluded that people would be better served by day centres working in partnership with supported and generic employment agencies and mainstream services such as Jobcentre Plus and WORKSTEP.[7] The importance of working in partnership with local employers has also been acknowledged in some areas.

2.4.8   Transition to work

We came across few examples of vocational courses or training that included support for the transition to work for younger people. Some special schools are reported to include work experience and vocational training in their curricula and are supporting pupils in jobs out of school hours,[92] but very few people with a learning disability enter employment straight from school.[64]

The Vocational Opportunities in Training for Employment (VOTE) in Northern Ireland aimed to improve the employment prospects of young people (aged between 18 and 25) with a range of impairments by offering courses and work placements that would lead to qualifications. While the report of four pilot projects does not always distinguish outcomes for people with a learning disability there were indications that VOTE was successful in generating employment for a small number of people (although no comparison data is available) and in terms of social inclusion. The project was also notable for the degree of partnership working between agencies.[78]

The Open Society Institute (OSI) monitoring report on access to education and employment for people with learning disabilities points to 'consistent messages' from research about what is going wrong with the transition system in relation to employment: it is not pursued as an option in transition planning and where it is, young people find a lack of personal support, poor transport and the same problems with benefits that affect adults in work.[64]

2.4.9 Future best practice for supporting people into work

The literature contains a number of messages about the best ways to support people with learning disabilities into work:

- training and preparation for work should be centred on the workplace to break the cycle of endless 'introductory' course
- supported employment agencies need guaranteed streams of funding
- more work needs to be done engaging employers and co-workers in the process of employing people with learning disabilities
- not all people want to move into open employment and many prefer the choice of a social firm or enterprise where they can feel more in control
- information and advice about jobs, employment support and benefits should be improved.

2.5 Further education

Further education is the third arm of a triad of services, along with day and employment services, which provide the bulk of publicly funded daytime support to people with learning disabilities. It can be 'an exciting and useful day activity for people with a learning disability'[*] and just over half of the further education colleges surveyed in 2000 said they enrolled students with profound and complex learning disabilities, although full-time provision was offered only at specialist colleges. The few opportunities that were identified for this group in the mainstream sector varied greatly in type, range and quality of provision.[79]

Despite the increasingly heavy usage by people with learning disabilities, despite poor information about what is available in some areas,[80] further education provision has failed to enhance their social inclusion because it usually takes place in segregated settings[2, 44] and because 'there is limited awareness of the needs of people with intellectual disabilities within the sector'.[64] Although people with learning disabilities do contribute as teachers of learning disability studies and professional courses in higher education settings;[81, 112] further education has come to be seen as a 'substitute' day service[1] and colleges sometimes operate as quasi-day centres with no real sense of purpose.[21]

Further education has also failed to provide career pathways in work,[2] despite a heavy emphasis on 'preparedness' through life skills courses,[**] with little thought given as to what will happen afterwards.[1] The OSI report concludes that 'many colleges still fail to provide clear teaching geared towards employment. There is a lack of a successful match between the skills and courses taught and the jobs people are successful at getting on the local jobs market'.[64] Despite the fragility of funding one study was able to report success factors for transition to work pro-

---

[*] *'Valuing People* – much achieved, much more to do: a summary report of inspections carried out in 2003/2004 of 12 social care services for people with learning disabilities', Commission for Social Care Inspection (www.csci.gsi.gov.uk).

[**] Some courses pursue non-vocational objectives such as, 'cognitive and personal development, as well as aesthetic and spiritual enrichment'.[113]

grammes, including the support of senior managers, an acknowledge-ment among support staff in all sectors that employment is a realistic goal for people with a learning disability, the use of learner-led training packages, and information on the impact of pay on benefits.[82]

Colleges and the local LSCs need to think about 'exit strategies' for people with a learning disability and to ensure that appropriate support services are available to help people get paid jobs. The consensus from the literature is that this sector needs to be more outcomes-focused and to emphasise routes to employment as the norm.[7]

Models of peer-supported learning offer a way to enhance the life-skills programmes that are the staple of further education courses for people with learning disabilities. One novel example is the Supported Learning Project, which was set up to support mothers with learning disabilities in their parenting by equipping them to take greater control of their lives (self-advocacy) and to strengthen their families by offer-ing peer support and personal development. Thirty-one mothers were recruited to the project, attending weekly meetings and support groups and accessing other activities according to their needs and preferences. The evaluation of the project says little about the outcomes in terms of the mothers' parenting skills or the effects on their families, but does draw the 'broad conclusions' that the learning opportunity offered by the project bolstered the mothers' confidence and that it raised their self-esteem.[83]

A review of the learning needs of people with learning and other disabilities in one English county made a number of recommendations with a wider relevance:[84]

- Use of person-centred planning should be advocated to guide both individual learning and strategic planning of education services.
- People should be encouraged to consider work as an option at an early stage and offered more work experience opportunities.
- Local authorities should offer a coordinated approach to providing advice about learning and work options, recognising the lead role of Connexions.
- Information about learning and work should be made more avail-able[80] and accessible.

- Advice from Jobcentre Plus and disability advisors needs to be supplemented with more information on the range of employment-related activities, self-employment and setting up a small business.
- There should be follow-up work done to track how people progress once they leave further education.
- Work should be done to raise awareness among service providers about access to work-based learning programmes
- There should be more sheltered employment places created, ensuring that this does not become yet another 'holding bay' with no progression.
- Work should be done with employers to help to challenge their misconceptions about the potential of disabled people.

These are all issues that have been noted by the Learning and Skills Development Agency (LSDA), the umbrella organisation for post-16 education and training. Since 2003, the LSDA has been involved in developing and supporting practice among adult and community learning providers to implement the Disability Discrimination Act 1995. This has involved action research[*] with a large number of further education providers across England, to address a number of central issues, including the following:

- developing appropriate learning programmes for adults with learning difficulties
- promoting progression and effective transition
- promoting access to employment through work experience
- promoting access to employment for adults with learning difficulties
- developing inclusive provision for people with profound and complex learning difficulties.

Two recent reviews in the field of further education have also reiterated many of the above issues, while heralding many changes to further education provision. *Through inclusion to excellence*, the review of strategic

---

[*] Work is still in progress, but see the following web link for more information (www.lsda.org.uk/dda/home.aspx).

planning and funding of provision for learners with learning difficulties and/or disabilities,[85] clarifies a strong commitment to the importance of progression to employment as a positive outcome for people with learning disabilities. The review notes that more emphasis should be placed on progression to employment and 'the acquisition of skills that enable disabled people to play a full and active part in their communities'.[85, p 3] It also highlights the value of direct experience in work, rather than training for work, and promotes the inclusion of supported employment agencies as key players in the provision of effective support. The Foster review of further education[86] recommends further development and change with a greater clarity of purpose and clarity of strategy. The report recommends a comprehensive set of reforms aimed at increasing the reputation and impact of further education, including a core focus on skills and employability.

2.6 Summary and conclusions

This research review has highlighted the following main themes relating to community-based day activities for people with learning disabilities.

- Community-based day activities encompass different forms of employment, further education, leisure and other types of 'without walls' provision that operate outside of day centres. Initiatives are varied but may be categorised in terms of their focus on: performing arts, places, relationships or as a means of opening up a wide range of opportunities.
- Despite a strong policy emphasis on modernisation of day services, it appears from the literature in this field that day activities are still based around day centres and that a large proportion of people with learning disabilities still use day centres on a regular basis.
- Although it is widely acknowledged that community-based provision affords opportunities for social inclusion and desegregation, some activities that take place in community settings are purposively segregated. It appears that the debate about social inclusion/exclusion for people with learning disabilities is more nuanced than is generally acknowledged and that doing an activity in a community setting

does not automatically ensure that an individual has contact with non-disabled people or is living an ordinary life.

- There are numerous barriers to the development of community-based day activities: lack of alternative provision; lack of effective partnerships between services and departments; difficulties in decision making; lack of time to understand and plan properly with individuals; benefits issues; and problems with transport. Self-advocates suggest that services should worry less about providing a menu of options and concentrate more on listening to what people say they want and meeting those needs in flexible ways.

- The modernisation agenda has provided a template for action and change by local authorities. As yet, there is very little written information available to help gauge the impact of these reforms, but early (and incomplete) indications are that progress is relatively slow overall and that significant structural problems still remain. There remains a need for sharing of good practice to avoid duplication of effort.

- Ingredients for effective change include: partnership with people and their families; leadership; cultural change in services; personalised planning with and for people; individualised funding and direct payments; 'smart' commissioning; staff development; and community capacity building.

- There has been, and still appears to be, a lack of clarity about the role and function of day activities. This may have contributed to the dearth of good quality, evaluative research on the impact of day services for people with learning disabilities.

In addition to the knowledge gap identified relating to role, function and impact of day activities, this review has indicated several other significant gaps in the literature. The first of these relates to the provision of day opportunities for people from minority ethnic communities, people with profound and multiple learning difficulties, and people in older and younger age categories, although the second phase of the Changing Days Programme did include three development sites working alongside people with complex needs, their families and staff, to improve day opportunities.[88] The needs of these groups need to be understood and budgeted for.[10] For example, the Choice Initiative demonstrated that communication is the essential starting point in addressing choice for people with a learning disability and high support needs. Those with profound or multiple learning difficulties or from minority ethnic groups tend to miss out on learning.

Summers and Jones[87] stress the importance of staff examining their own beliefs and attitudes as part of training for working with people with learning difficulties from minority ethnic communities. Training should include teaching and discussion around specific cultural beliefs and norms so staff can begin to develop a framework for working cross-culturally.

The Changing Days team argued that the same principles for changing day opportunities for people from disadvantaged groups start with person-centred planning, focus on abilities and give top priority to developing effective communication.[4, 44]

Many of the themes that are threaded through this Research Review are reflected in the parallel practice survey report. For instance, it was evident from the practice survey that many local authorities are still struggling to move away from large, congregate settings. However, where good progress was being made, this was based on an individualised and person-centred approach. Self-advocates in the regional workshops also echoed the desire expressed in this Research Review to have meaningful activities, such as paid work, through which they could make a contribution to society.

However, there are new themes emerging from practice, which outstrip the published literature. The practice survey explores and reflects on some examples of areas where a person-centred approach is changing the way services are configured. There are also examples of day centre staff moving over successfully in some areas into supported employment work, and people with learning disabilities taking on roles and activities that earn them respect and value in their communities. People with learning disabilities, like other disabled people[48] have a right to choice and control over their own lives, and this report has revealed that day services alone cannot enable them to have that autonomy. A joined-up approach will couple person-centred planning with an individualised budget, good community network building and individualised support. All these things are necessary in order for people with learning disabilities to 'have a good day', and future research must take a more holistic view of people's lives.

Practice Survey

3.1 Preface

This practice survey report is part of a knowledge review aimed at "identifying what has, and what has not contributed to the successful provision of community-based day activities for all people with learning disabilities".[104] The review was commissioned by the Social Care Institute for Excellence (SCIE) and has been undertaken by the Foundation for People with Learning Disabilities (FPLD) and Norah Fry Research Centre (NFRC) working in partnership. A separate research review report[108] sits alongside this report to make up the full knowledge review.

The practice survey team included two people with learning disabilities, two family carers and two service commissioners working alongside 6 researchers from FPLD and NFRC. Carlisle People First undertook two pieces of work on the team's behalf. The team set out to "find, describe and consider" examples of current good practice that are not written down and captured in the existing research (SCIE, undated). The survey focused on England, Wales and Northern Ireland, but examples from Scotland are also included in this report where they illustrate practice not commonly seen elsewhere.

The examples given in this document are from services followed up through either telephone interviews or visits. The sites/services that were visited are referred to as Areas 1 - 8 and a brief profile of each can be found in Appendix 10. The services followed up by telephone are referred to by name and their contact information can be found in Appendix 11.

3.2 Background

3.3 What is 'a good day'?

Previous evidence indicated that significant numbers of people with learning disabilities were spending their days using services that were provided in congregate settings, not encouraging open employment[94] and which were placing various limits on the lives of the people they served.[100, 101, 107, 110] An estimated 20,000 people with learning disabilities were thought not to be accessing any supported day activities at all.[102]

Policies such as *Valuing People* in England[96] and *The same as you* in Scotland[106] have led the way in promoting person-centred approaches and more meaningful, community-based lives for people with learning disabilities, including improved support to obtain paid jobs. The emphasis has been on people being supported to take their place as citizens, participating as full and equal members of society.

This practice survey examines what difference the policies have made in practice, asking whether people with learning disabilities are literally 'having a good day?'.

The research review report that accompanies this document outlines the policies underpinning the move to community-based day activities. In brief, 'having a good day' is defined in policy as being about people with learning disabilities spending their days:

- working
- in education or training
- volunteering
- participating in leisure activities, arts and hobbies
- socialising with friends.

All people, irrespective of the level of support they need, will be:

- undertaking activities that have a purpose
- in ordinary places, doing things that most members of the community would be doing

- doing things that are uniquely right for them, with support that meets their individual and specific requirements and overcomes inequalities
- meeting local people, developing friendships, connections and a sense of belonging.

3.4 How the practice survey was structured

Detailed information about how the survey was carried out can be found in Appendix 8. In summary:

- Criteria for selecting services were firmed up following five regional workshops with participants, by invitation, from self-advocacy and carer organisations, services and consultancy groups, all identified as local champions for community-based day provision.
- The workshops also helped identify services and projects in each region that were considered to be delivering 'good' community-based opportunities and support. Others were identified through the literature search for the research review, networking with national service development and consultancy organisations, searching the Foundation for People with Learning Disabilities (FPLD) Choice Forum (an interactive discussion website), and calling for suggestions through national advertising and media coverage.
- Carlisle People First used their local networks to identify potential good practice examples in one region where a workshop had not proved viable. The organisation also contacted large advocacy organisations in each region covered by the survey to hear from people with learning disabilities about the community-based services they would recommend.
- Services and projects were contacted by email or telephone and further information gathered using a pro forma based on the criteria for inclusion. The pro forma can be found in Appendix 9. Services were excluded from the survey at this point if they did not fully meet the criteria.
- Eight services were selected for more in-depth study. A team of four people spent a day with each service using a structured approach to gather information from a range of different stakeholders. The team included a researcher and three associates – a person with learning

disabilities, a family carer and a commissioner – to provide a balanced and informed view from a variety of complementary perspectives. The information collecting format for the visits can be found in Appendix 9.

All the work for the 'Having A Good Day' Project took place over a six-month period from June to December 2005, including the writing up. The practice survey needed to draw on information uncovered through the research review and the initial workshops. The search for best practice services/sites needed to happen before decisions could be made about which ones to visit. We were ambitious in our plans and, in reality, our approach had to be adapted to fit the time frame. For such a large piece of work, across the UK, it was simply not enough time. We know that there are other services doing good, innovative community-based work that have not been mentioned in this report.

3.5 Criteria for inclusion

The criteria for including services in the survey were based on the main messages from national policy combined with the perspectives of people participating in the workshops. A long list identified 51 qualities that 'good' community-based day activities would demonstrate (listed in Appendix 8). From these, 15 were singled out as key areas of interest. For a service to be included in the survey we expected it to be supporting people to:

- connect with and do things alongside people for reasons other than having a learning disability
- contribute to society – by undertaking valued roles (for example, working)
- build and maintain friendships
- lead and be in control of what happens
- use ordinary community places and facilities outside the 'learning disability' world
- do things alongside people who do not have a learning disability
- use places that are in keeping with ordinary patterns of life
- make use of settings specific to their cultural preferences

- do things based on the person's own desires and aspirations
- do things that give shape to their lives, and that make sense for them; things that are meaningful and purposeful for them
- make choices and decisions, and fully participate in doing things
- do things with the right amount and type of support that they need
- be as independent as possible

and we expected that the service would be:

- monitoring delivery and outcomes for individuals
- reasonably confident about its sustainability (that is, with reasonable confidence about its funding base).

3.6   Services included

The search generated 161 suggestions of services and initiatives that might be relevant to the survey. Of these, 30 did not meet the inclusion criteria and 78 could not be followed up by telephone or email because of combined difficulties around contacting managers and research time available. The majority of these were small voluntary sector services and/or work training projects that appeared, on paper, to be similar to others we had already contacted. Our aim was to achieve a spread of good practice examples across employment, learning and leisure-focused initiatives, and including both newly created and 'modernised' services.

Detailed information was gathered by telephone or email from 53 services, projects and initiatives all delivering community-based opportunities and support. Research teams subsequently visited eight services that appeared to be achieving best practice. Services referred to by name in this report have given their permission and their contact details are listed in Appendix 10 (sites/services visited) and Appendix 11 (services telephoned).

No service is perfect, and the best community-based provision is evolving and changing as lessons are being learnt from practice. There is not a single 'model' of delivery that can be held up as 'the best way' or 'the right way'. We found a large number of services that are delivering some good community-based opportunities and support in the midst of more traditional provision. We did not find any service where we could say that *everything* being done is 'best practice', an example for others to follow. Where services are mentioned in this report we have identified the specific aspects of their provision that stood out to us as good community-based practice.

Service managers and local authority policy makers were naturally keen to tell us about what they are doing and the 'vision' they are putting into action. Our visits gathered more in-depth information about how that vision is being implemented. As might be expected when researching a new service direction, implementation did not always match the vision. Some services had little evidence to support their positive descriptions of what was being achieved. While many supported employment services had been formally evaluated, often linked to contract requirements, few of the general community-based services had. The practice survey did not, and could not undertake detailed evaluation of services or of their outcomes. Community-based services need to give greater attention to evaluation of their achievements, and disseminating the findings for the benefit of others undertaking the journey.

The concept of 'community-based day activities' encompasses a huge array of approaches, settings, service providers and areas of life. It is a very wide brief for a short piece of research: a six-month time frame cannot do it justice. This survey has scratched the surface and developed a snapshot of good practice, but greater exploration is needed.

3.7 Findings

3.7.1 *What* people are doing

Connecting with and doing things alongside people for reasons other than having a learning disability

There is ample evidence that people are moving from five days a week using a single service to a pattern that is far more varied. People are increasingly supported by a mixture of services during the course of a week, doing a variety of different things. This man's experience appeared fairly typical:

'Mondays and Tuesdays I'm here [in nursery project] all day. We sell the plants, and we always do the grass outside – the hedge and that. Besides that, I go Wednesday and Thursday to catering, at the church. I go with the people I work with. Fridays, I always go to see my friends at the day centre, and in the afternoon I go to dancing. That's exercise and things like that.'

(person with learning disabilities, Area 1)

Leisure and sports-focused initiatives in particular are opening up opportunities where people *choose* to come together to do things because they share an interest in what is on offer. Many of these have *open* referral systems: people can simply turn up if they want to take part in what's on offer. Several grew out of self-advocacy groups when people decided that they wanted the chance to do evening leisure activities as well as meeting to discuss shared issues. Others have developed during day service modernisation, often extending the level of provision available for existing day service users. We found little evidence that evening and weekend leisure provision developed by statutory services is being used strategically to extend support to people with learning disabilities who were *not* previously 'in the system'.

Some services are helping people to build up their confidence in using a community setting alongside others with learning disabilities, but are then supporting individuals to branch out on their own there. We heard evidence that such deliberate strategies are beginning to yield positive results.

In **South Gloucestershire**, the learning disabilities service funded a leisure and sports coordinator post within the council's mainstream community services. The aim of the post was to support people into integrated provision, and there have been some successes. For example, 10 people were supported to use the local golf club and receive training from the golf pro. Two were then supported to join the golf club in their own right.

Most of the leisure and sports initiatives contacted, however, were unable to offer the same opportunities to people who need high levels of support unless accompanied by their own support worker or personal assistant. Individualised support is not available to many people unless they have individualised funding, for example through Independent Living Fund (ILF) monies, a direct or indirect payment.

People who need higher levels of support are being grouped together because of the level of support and specialised equipment or facilities they need, rather than because of a shared interest or goal. The settings being used may be more community-based, and the size of groups may be smaller, but the indications are that people with profound and multiple learning disabilities are predominantly accessing just one service in a week, and it is likely to be a segregated, congregate one. Unequal opportunities persist. This is explored more in the course of this report.

Contributing – undertaking valued roles, working and having a career

> 'Kevin enjoys going to work. It's the first thing he says when he opens his eyes: 'I've got work to do'. He tells everybody about his work.'
> (personal support worker, Area 4)

In the 14 employment services we contacted we heard about several hundred people who had been helped to move into paid work. In Area 6 the local scheme had helped 30 people into paid employment in one year, while supporting another 130 people already working. There was an office assistant, assembly worker, caterer and play assistant, someone employed at John Lewis, another by the BBC. Job searching was assisted by a network that include leading employers, the local council and NHS Trusts. Area 4 has 110 people in paid jobs of 16 hours or more. With the introduction of tax credits people had felt more confident about giving up their income-related benefits. Overall, however, fears about 'losing benefits' was a theme that resonated from across services.

All the supported employment agencies contacted were using Training in Systematic Instruction for skills teaching, but it was not at all evident in other types of service. All the agencies were also using vocational profiling and were fading their support once people were placed in jobs. Continued low level support was being offered so that people could progress and establish careers.

> 'Everyone breathes a sigh of relief when they get a person with a learning disability a job. Job done! But it's not job done. There's the continuation of the support, the extension of the work placement so

they don't become bored. So the concept of career can be important, and they do get extended.'

(deputy director, Area 2)

Although there were several examples of people receiving ongoing job support funded through Access to Work monies, agencies identified issues around providing long-term support 'on the job' for people who need it. This is seen as a consequence of a 'high volume, low cost' emphasis in most external funding streams, and outcomes focused on jobs of 16 hours per week or more. It has required agencies to be creative in finding ways to achieve sustained support. It has meant that many supported employment agencies are not able to serve people who need higher levels of ongoing support.

We were heartened to discover a few supported employment schemes and small social enterprises that are supporting people with more complex needs. Most supported employment schemes emphasise that it's about getting the job-matching process right. The numbers of people accessing such opportunities are small overall, but they demonstrate that work really can be an option with the right support.

Linkage Green is a social enterprise where 7-10 people are supported to work each day taking care of a county class bowling green and cafe in Mablethorpe. The business runs seven days a week. The majority of the people have high support needs. They match people's interest and skills to tasks. One person, for example, works as a 'table supplies controller' filling condiments for one hour a day, three days a week, paid at the National Minimum Wage.

In areas where there is little supported employment provision or where the local supported employment agency is at capacity, day services are taking a more active role around preparing people for work. Day service staff are developing new skills and taking on new employment-related roles as part of day service modernisation. The picture is patchy, however, and the role of day services in relation to employment does not appear to have a strategic push in many areas. Although impressive, the figures quoted above for people with learning disabilities obtaining paid work in Areas 6 and 4 are still only around 10% of all those who use day services in those areas.

The growing work-related role of day service staff is seen very clearly in the development of social firms and cooperatives as a part of day service modernisation strategies. Where these have developed into self-financing businesses they are viewed positively by local planners. We found many social firms that are aiming to develop into small businesses, and a few that had already succeeded (such as Linkage Green above, which has won a business award).

Beyond the supported employment schemes and social firms most people using community-based day services have very leisure-focused days. Work appears to be seen as just another choice rather than the core of daily life it is for most adults in our society. People are described as having 'busy lives' with difficulty fitting work in. There are issues about whether staff in day services expect people to work and contribute to society, and see that they can.

Self-employment (micro-enterprise) has begun to be explored more in very recent years as a way into paid work for some people, and it is encouraging to find areas where specific training is being offered to help people take that step.

In **Norfolk** a partnership between the Learning and Skills Council (LSC), local authority and Norwich City College has led to an initiative to develop social firms and social enterprises. A community interest company is being set up that can raise shares and capital investment. As well as work to generate new social firms there has been a course for people with learning disabilities about micro-enterprise. A total of £5,000 of Learning Disability Development Fund money has been used to offer 'start-up' grants of up to £500 to people. So far, four people have received this support – a musical entertainer, a market stallholder selling children's clothes, an ebay art emporium and a dog walking service.

Linked to a direct payment, self-employment may be a way forward for people who have not been able to get the level of support they need to find work because of problems meeting eligibility criteria for services.

'With regard to work opportunities, it would have to be self-employment as my son has complex needs, but we haven't ruled out, for example, a dog walking business or maybe to caretake the local village hall. With 2:1 support he can try most anything that is within his ability, and there's nothing stopping us trying anything that we think he would enjoy or succeed with. We aren't bound by the restrictions that organisations have to follow, like risk assessments. We learn from our son – what makes sense for him, what he enjoys and what he's good at – and because he's got support we aren't limited with what we can try.'

(family carer at Workshop 1)

We found just one Supported Employment Scheme that is providing a targeted service for people with higher functioning Autistic Spectrum Disorder or Asperger's syndrome (Aspire, part of Fife Council's **EmployAbility Team** in Scotland). Self-employment may be a helpful alternative route.

Having a respected role in society is not exclusively about paid work. There were positive examples of voluntary work and charitable activity:

'I've got a couple of disabled friends at a swimming club I attend on a Friday night. I am a helper, and I help disabled children of many ages to swim. It's a job, I intend to do it – without money.'

(person with learning disabilities, Area 3)

We found people with learning disabilities working in teams alongside park warders contributing to public projects and regeneration, others enjoying volunteering in cafes attached to museums or historic houses. Volunteers who received training in media skills through taking part in a local community radio station, set up by Pure Innovations in Stockport (Area 6), had set up an audio-visual suite to provide resources for their local council. Direct payments are enabling some people to contribute in this way as well. In Appendix 12 Tom Cowen from York describes how he has raised a significant amount of money for charity with the support of a personal assistant, secured through a direct payment.

We heard, however, of people who are undertaking voluntary work that is self-perpetuating or, to all intents and purposes, unpaid work.

Many are using small work training projects with unclear links to job-seeking support. We also, however, found several services with more deliberate approaches where voluntary work and training schemes are used as a stepping stone to paid employment, with job-seeking support linked in.

The **Weavers Restaurant Trust** in East London provides accredited training for work in hospitality and catering, IT and adult literacy. They are open to anyone from across London. Among other things, they offer NVQ courses in food preparation and customer service with a four-week trial for people to decide if the training meets their needs. Applicants for other courses are assessed for their individual needs. Once people have achieved accreditation they are helped to find work. Job search support is built in.

Despite the encouraging examples, however, we found few areas with sufficient supported employment provision to meet demand from young people in transition from schools and colleges. In Areas 2 and 3 projects were based around schools, but this appears relatively uncommon. Where employment tasters and job-seeking support *is* being offered to young people they are more likely to move straight from school or college into work.

Area 2 has an established range of opportunities and training provision and ample ways of moving people from one to the other. They work with young people at the transition stage in schools to plant seeds about work early on:

'... my view is that it always has to be an enabling process, with our student/trainee at the core of that. All of us make changes in our career. People with learning disabilities are no different. We plant that seed at age 14, and then at 16 we start to work for them within school. We do careers tasters. Nobody can make an informed choice unless they experience and know.' (manager, Area 2)

> The organisation has enough specialist staff to ensure that people with learning disabilities do not get 'stuck' at any stage. We met a man who had trained in one of the high street cafes run by the society and then moved on to look for a job. He now has a regular job at a restaurant.

Building and maintaining friendships

'You need your friend, because a friend is most important….'
(person with learning disabilities, Area 1)

Supporting people to have a good social life is a key role in any community-based service.[111] We found many examples of evening social groups, often run by people with learning disabilities (with support), that give an opportunity for people to go out to pubs, clubs, the cinema, restaurants and other places together. They are about people having fun together and spending time with friends. The majority are facilitated by voluntary sector organisations, with some badged as 'short-break' provision, but several statutory sector day services are also actively managing their staffing to provide support for people to meet in the evenings and do fun things together in ordinary community places.

> In **Stratford**, Warwickshire, the local authority day service has moved from a large day centre to four smaller community bases. There is also a base-less service that supports people to do things directly from their homes. The staffing for that service, which operates during the day and some evenings, is mainly being achieved by actively managing the hours of staff working from the four bases. Four staff spend at least some of the week with the service, alongside its one part-time member of staff.

Such social opportunities mainly take place in groups with other people with learning disabilities. They help people to maintain existing friendships and to meet other people with learning disabilities, but more deliberate strategies are needed to help people build friendships with people beyond the 'learning disability' network. As one manager pointed out, it takes time:

'This work can be slow to show results. It's much easier to show more activity happening in someone's life than it is to show new relationships growing.... Funders want specific and measurable results within a timescale.'

(voluntary sector manager)

Clearly new social patterns are emerging for many people, building from contact with family and neighbours to time spent with friends from the local community, the workplace and leisure activities. The people we met who are in open employment had all benefited hugely from the social aspects of work going, for example, to karaoke nights with colleagues, and meeting up with people from Eastern Europe in a recycling plant.

It is also clear, however, that people who need *higher* levels of support are rarely getting the chance to socialise in the evenings and at weekends. Availability of support appears to be the key issue.

The survey shows very clearly the importance of black and minority ethnic advocacy organisations in creating opportunities for people to spend time and build friendships with others who share their culture and faith. Most social provision we found targeted to people from black and mibority ethnic communities had evolved from advocacy and mapping projects set up to 'reach in' to people within local ethnic communities.

Leading and being in control of what happens

Being in control can mean both having choices and autonomy in your own life, but also having a voice in organising and planning activities and support services more generally. As far as individual choices are concerned, direct and indirect payments, and self-directed support[97] are all about people being in control of what happens in their life. The original 'in-control' pilot sites in England are of interest in terms of the choices that people who are 'in control' are making about their day activities and the consequent impact on services. While the number of people involved in the in-control pilot is small it is clear that people are choosing to spend time doing ordinary, community-based activities. Some have reduced their use of day centres as a result. With a personal assistant, made possible through a direct or indirect payment, people can do the things that they want to do – so far these appear from the pilot sites to be mainly leisure and home focused.

There is a clear emerging theme about pressure on community care purchasing budgets resulting from increased take-up of direct payments. As yet local authorities do not seem to be taking a strategic approach and deliberately transferring money from day service budgets into purchasing budgets to help make more individualised services and support happen.

> '... although we have a pretty good direct payment scheme, this doesn't really cohere with our commissioning and decommissioning activity.'
>
> (commissioning manager)

Money released through day service modernisation is also being used to help meet 'savings' targets set by local authorities. It's a challenge to extend direct payments, and thereby control, to more people in such a climate.

Looking beyond the individual, to participation in planning and organising, involvement of people with learning disabilities and family carers on management groups, advisory groups and boards is quite common. **Grapevine**, a voluntary sector provider in Coventry, has people with learning disabilities occupying 50 per cent of the places on its board. It supports people to 'develop, lead and organise their own projects and activities' and aims to encourage mutual support. There is a campaigns team, a health promotion team, and D:vine – a group of young learning diabled people who run nightclub nights.

Managers and policy makers have developed some creative strategies for listening to what people want on an ongoing basis. In Area 5, money is being given to develop participation groups in each locality base. In Area 4, video testimonies of people's wishes had been made, and were used to inspire and plan services. The authority delivered their 'partnership in practice agreement', setting out the direction for services, in video format. In Area 7, People First works across day services to help people advocate and influence day-to-day choices and longer-term service development. It is clear that services are, in the main, approaching involvement with thought:

'My experience tells me that if you involve people from the word GO it might take you longer to get to your solutions and outcomes, but those outcomes tend to be much higher quality. So that's what we're doing.'

(commissioner, Area 2)

The influence of self-advocacy groups in developing and running evening leisure opportunities has been significant. We also found examples where daytime 'drop-ins' run by people with learning disabilities are being developed as part of day service modernisation, but often in a segregated base. It is not clear whether this 'clubhouse' model really is shifting power and control into the hands of people with learning disabilities, and deserves further exploration.

In **Area 5** people have moved from two large day centres to use smaller community bases. There is also a building – a 'drop-in' – which is run by self-advocates. They have their own keys and a committee to organise the activities. The social services vision statement says: 'We want you to have real power and take the power away from us'.

Parents have also had an important impact, initiating and leading new developments in some areas.

The **Welsh Initiative for Supported Employment (WISE)** was set up in 1984 by a group of parents who believed in giving people with learning disability the opportunity to work. It's now a registered charity, a limited company and a community cooperative. It serves around 280 people. Four of the Trustees are parents.

Families have also, however, had an impact in a number of areas in curbing plans to develop community-based services. The interplay between political decision making and the influence of parents and families has clearly affected the shape and pace of developments. In some areas implementation of day service modernisation plans have become long drawn-out and prolonged. In the London Borough of Hackney, one of the original sites in the Changing Days Project, the plan to move out from one of the existing day centres took nine years to achieve. The issue is illustrated by the comments of a local authority day service manager:

'There's one old centre left. I wasn't allowed to shut it. It's empty much of the day.'

The parents we met on visits, however, had been totally won over to new and individual ways of working, largely to do with the increased opportunities their son or daughter had for a meaningful life. Many echoed the following sentiment from the parent of a young person still in the transition years from school:

'It's been very positive, and it's given us an insight to encourage him to do the things he's capable of. The more independent he becomes the easier it'll be for us, especially in later years. It'll give him more confidence as well. You should have seen his face when he first learnt to make a cup of tea and could bring it to us!'

(family carer, Area 2)

Partnership with parents is more likely to be achieved if services start when people are young. Parental expectations, at that stage, are rightly high: they do not want large congregate settings for their son or daughter, and want them to fulfil their individual ambitions. Most parents want to be involved because they care about the person; services *need* parents and families to be involved because they have information and ideas to offer.

In many areas of the UK, involvement in strategy and service planning has become paid work for some people with learning disabilities – a very valued day 'activity'.

Mencap in Northern Ireland has a 'learning disabilities equalities officer' post that is presently filled by two people with learning disabilities. They provide invaluable insights about their own experiences, helping other people to make informed choices about supported employment, and helping employers to work more effectively with people with learning disabilities.

In Essex, **Listening To Us** was set up as a social firm in 1998, employing a team of people with a learning disability to undertake consultations, develop and deliver training, plan and run events, and speak at conferences. The team broadened out to work with training cooperatives, supporting users to take more control and leadership. Listening To Us specialise in promoting inclusion and participation through person-centred approaches. Since 2004, the team has been employed directly by Mencap and now has a national rather than regional role. Team members continue to have an active role in the success of the business. They are involved in making decisions and running the organisation, and continue to carry out work for a range of organisations.

In the West Midlands, **People First** undertook paid work for the *Valuing People* Support Team acting as 'mystery shoppers' to find out about the direct payments schemes run by local councils. At the end they gave a presentation to managers from the local authorities to influence the development of the schemes.

3.7.2 *Where* people are doing things

Using ordinary community places and facilities outside the 'learning disability' world

It may be true, as one manager said, that *'Community is an experience, and not a location'* but community is something to integrate into, not be separate from, and that *is* about location. We found that where large, segregated day centres have been closed, the move has most often been to smaller bases where there is designated space for people with learning disabilities to use.

> In Area 7, six teams have moved out from the two old day centres and now operate from rooms within ordinary community centres around the borough. Some people have started to help with the running and upkeep of one of the centres others have got involved in other ordinary activities running at the centres.

We were told of 'community bases' in church halls, community centres, healthy living centres, further education (FE) colleges, a cricket club, at an allotment, in refurbished offices and shops, amongst others. A strong theme that has emerged is the development of arts and theatre groups that have broken away from day services to take on a life of their own, using community settings to meet, exhibit and perform (for example, the No Limit Theatre Company in Sunderland).

We heard of some exciting developments in partnership with community groups, and of 'win-win' deals being brokered with a range of community partners in order to create accessible space within community buildings. Some of these are summarised below.

The Alumwell Poject

> When neighbourhood housing offices based on local estates in the Walsall district were being disposed of the day services commissioner stepped in and took two, for free. A partnership has been developed with the Alumwell Residents Trust to develop one building as a community centre for local people. The Trust has used funding from the Fair Share lottery fund, administered through the Birmingham Foundation, to renovate the building. A local councilor is very involved with the Residents Trust, and a local resident is pushing for it to be really inclusive. There are exciting possibilities.

The Maidenhead Sensory Zone

> Local day services worked with leisure services in Maidenhead to refurbish a squash court shower room in the town's leisure centre. It's been turned into the 'Sensory Zone' using Learning Disability Development Fund (LDDF) capital money, and is used

by people with learning disabilities two days a week and open to any members of the public the rest of the time. Subsequently, a new accessible toilet and changing facility was opened within the leisure centre next to the Sensory Zone, again open to anyone. The partnership has started to have spin-off benefits, with one person now working in the leisure centre shop.

Holy Bones, Leicester
Leicester City Council social care services have contracted a local Sikh organisation to deliver a service for Asian young people with learning disabilities in transition to adulthood. The service runs over seven days a week, based from the Sikh community centre.

Depending on how they are used, community bases (even if just designated space within a shared building) still run the risk of replicating the segregated world of day centres. Services emphasised that the intention is to use a small base as a 'jumping off point' to easier and greater community integration. Some are achieving that more than others. One young woman we met, for instance, was using a small group 'base' in a former respite unit. She was alongside much older people with whom she had little in common, and felt she had lost links with old friends and interests. Her mother, however, saw it as a better alternative than her daughter being at home isolated from others, as well as being a break for herself.

Small bases can be a 'second best' strategy if the services operating out of them are not actively and deliberately managed to do just that – support people to be 'out of them'. They do, as several managers pointed out, give families the confidence that there is a 'fall-back', and without that security many of the managers we spoke to are doubtful that they would have got so far down the road towards community-based provision. A *shared* base at least gives the opportunity for contact with other people.

More worryingly, we found learning disability services that are actively commissioning their *own* new buildings. They will need to apply very deliberate strategies to prevent segregation. Some of this development is undoubtedly linked to the availability of capital monies through the LDDF and local authorities. Local developments in Shropshire are mapped out in the box below and illustrate how capital monies *can* be used creatively to achieve inclusive bases in shared community buildings.

Shropshire

Shropshire embarked on day service modernisation in the early 1990s. Some people were travelling for three hours or more to get to a day centre; more local provision was needed. Three local bases were initially developed. A Social Services Inspectorate (SSI) inspection in 2001 then recommended the approach be extended. A total of £800,000 of capital money was allocated by the local authority and, in all, 16 bases with their own teams of staff have been created. All three of the large day centres will have closed by the end of 2006. People with high support needs receive an integrated service. Capital money has been used to ensure that the new community bases are accessible and have appropriate equipment. One community centre had a changing bed and hoist installed into the football changing room ("it works well"); a personal care area was funded and built at Ellesmere Town Hall in return for reduced rental for the rooms people use; three new community centres are being funded through the Private Finance Initiative (PFI) programme and the service will be using part of these new community buildings. Most of the bases are shared community buildings and it's mostly local people who use them. Staff teams are tapping into local things that are happening and supporting people to take part. This has all resulted in people having a more valued and respected role in their communities.

In retrospect, the Shropshire manager believes that all the bases should have been developed for joint, rather than sole use as this has led to better outcomes. Other services have experienced constraints linked to running a building, as the manager below expresses:

'Our problem is having to run a drop-in centre – if we weren't do-ing that it would free capacity for more community-based time ... having to provide safe levels of staff cover for the centre impacts on everyone's work.'

Three community-based services (apart from employment services) were found to operate entirely with just an office base for staff, although we found several more 'outreach' or 'community' teams that are part of larger day services, many in the throes of modernisation. One service in particular, for people with high support needs in Norfolk, stands out as unique because of its size and the needs of the people it serves. Some key features of the service are described in the box below.

Area 8 (Community Support team, Norfolk County Council)
Following the closure of Little Plumstead Hospital, Norfolk County Council established a service to support people moving from the hospital. The Community Support Team now give individualised support to 92 people. Each person receives one-to-one support in the community to socialise, join clubs, undertake leisure activities and keep up with friendships. Each person is helped to decide how they want to spend their time and people receive varying amounts of support, most commonly three days weekly. People can choose to be supported at the weekend or in the evening and to take natural breaks away from home. There is no day centre base but a wide range of community locations are visited from home according to what the person chooses.

Norfolk and Shropshire are unusual. Overall the survey indicates that the pattern of provision for people with profound and multiple learning disabilities is more buildings-based, and more segregated. Conversely, for some people who are said to challenge services and who find group settings difficult direct payments appear to be opening up *more* com-munity-based opportunities. But, we are left wondering how many are receiving such tailor-made, individualised services and whether most people who challenge services are still using traditional day services, or none at all? This deserves further exploration.

The pattern for people from black and minority ethnic groups appears to be one of under-representation within community-based day and employment services when compared with local demographic information. The survey showed, however, that many managers do not have working knowledge of local demographics that suggests that meeting the needs of people from black and minority ethnic groups is still not very high on the agenda.

Having reliable transport is necessary to do the things that you want to do in most local communities. People want transport that they can trust, where they feel safe, and which they can manage by themselves if they can. We found a number of initiatives that are supporting people to travel independently. In **Hounslow** people with learning disabilities are employed to act as travel buddies for other people. In Norfolk car ownership has been pursued for one in every three people using the community-based service by using the mobility element of people's benefits. There are no large buses and all support workers are drivers. There is plentiful evidence that services are thinking creatively about transport and travelling – but it is matched by continuing frustrations, particularly about managers not having direct control of transport budgets and local public transport options being poor. This was reflected in a progress review of a new community-based service:

> Travel and transport arrangements are the most difficult to get right and yet are fundamental to providing day support.

For community-based services, operating in ordinary community facilities, influencing the way other people in those settings communicate with people with learning disabilities is a significant challenge. We found a number of projects, mainly grown from advocacy organisations and involving people with learning disabilities in delivery, that are working to shape and change how public facilities and services communicate.

The **Positive Futures Team** in Nottingham is a partnership involving the local authority, primary care trusts (PCTs), Mencap, Nottinghamshire Healthcare NHS Trust and the Home Farm Trust. Among other things their 'easy info group' has been working with local libraries, the Police and the witness care unit, education, housing and leisure services to improve their information. The group, of people with learning disabilities, check out the information and act as advisers.

Better Days in Newcastle supports people with learning disabilities to work with a range of organisations to break down barriers to inclusion. Their training group, of people with learning disabilities, deliver sessions that aim to raise awareness of the needs of people with learning disabilities. They have worked with staff at the civic centre, a local leisure centre, a health centre, and local museums and libraries.

Alongside people who do not have a learning disability

Participating in things alongside people who do not have a learning disability is a first step towards integration and real community inclusion.

We met the mother of someone labelled as having 'severe challenging behaviour'. With a direct payment, he is now supported individually in the community and has joined a local gym. Staff and other people at the gym have got to know him and greet his enthusiastic 'thumbs up' sign as he goes in for his evening swim. The private gym offered group membership to all the support workers who accompany him so that the activity is affordable.

Many services were able to give examples where people had been supported to join in activities alongside other local people, as members of the golf club, in healthy walking groups, litter picking teams, computer classes, a yoga group, to name but a few. We were encouraged that several of the managers we talked to are conscious of, and using clear strategies to build inclusion:

'With community inclusion one of the really important things is to use places on a regular basis, get to know staff there and they get to know us.'

(manager, Area 5)

But it is not a consistently positive picture. One commissioner, for example, told us about a group taking place in an ordinary public leisure centre with little connection to other people who use the centre. Direct support workers need to know and practice the strategies too.

Having a job and being alongside work colleagues naturally opens the door to new connections and relationships. A hotel supervisor we met during one site visit illustrates this well. She had developed a very good and positive relationship with a person with learning disabilities working in her team.

'Everyone went out of their way to make him feel welcome, but I think I just took a couple of steps more than everyone else. I got to know him well, and he started trusting me and the ones he would see on a daily basis.'

Her friendship and support proved a real help. She noticed that the employee's work was not bringing him into enough contact with other workers and so she advocated on his behalf to have his duties changed. Supporting people to develop their community connections is very much about recognising good, natural support and nurturing it. This includes stepping back at the right point, and allowing other people to get involved. The job coach had done just that, leaving her contact number as back up.

Joining further or adult education classes and courses provides another opportunity for people to meet other local residents who have an interest in learning the same thing. People with learning disabilities enjoy student life in colleges. We found only rare examples, however, of people with learning disabilities using mainstream college classes. People are largely accessing segregated provision specifically for people with learning disabilities. One manager's comments illustrate the situation well:

'We look to enrol people on mainstream courses if we can, as the first option. We are frequently told 'no, there's a course for people with learning disabilities'.

Lack of resources to provide individualised support for people in classes was commonly cited as the problem. We found *little* evidence of services deliberately seeking integrated opportunities and forcing the issue with education providers. There is also little evidence that people with more profound or complex disabilities access college or adult education classes at all. There were two exceptions that stood out, described below.

Norfolk

As a pathfinder site (see below) the LSC has been working with the local authority and Norwich City College to develop and design a 'skills for the job' curriculum. People will be able to access mainstream courses, just the parts that they need in order to fulfil their curriculum requirements. It will overcome many of the barriers around assessment and accessible learning that have existed to date.

Leicestershire Adult Learning Service

This transitions project is based at Rawlins, a community college in Leicestershire. The 'Transition Learning Programme' is a funding partnership between the local Adult Learning Service, LSC, social services, Connexions and health services. It is a 30 hours a week, 38-week provision for people with complex needs. Learning takes place for 16 hours per week and is mapped to pre-entry curriculum. People can attend for up to three years, and receive social care support to enable them to participate in the educational programme.

Targeted work is needed to identify what is happening and what is working in the Further and adult education sector. The LSC in England is currently funding a number of pathfinder projects aiming to develop and improve local provision so that young people do not have to leave their local area to access FE. The findings from these projects will hopefully demonstrate new ways of supporting people with learning disabilities to access educational opportunities.

Previously we discussed the theme of services developing bases within buildings shared by other people. Where the building is actually owned by the service the intention often cited is to open it up for use by others. This will bring people into contact with other users of the buildings, which over time may enable new connections to form. But, for this to really yield benefits deliberate strategies are needed: services need to actively manage relationships and create opportunities in their shared buildings. In Shropshire, for example, the team in one base set up a computer class and opened it up to local residents so that it became a mixed group. Many services said that they would welcome information that demonstrates a range of successful strategies that staff could use.

Places that are in keeping with ordinary patterns of life

We heard about people being supported to do things in a wide range of ordinary places at ordinary times of the day and evening, including a DJ training course, nightclubs, real jobs in a wide range of settings, projects in public parks and shopping areas, and sports centres, leisure centres, libraries, pubs and more. These places did not have to be specially created for the purpose. We know, however, that some places are more accessible and welcoming than others, both in terms of physical access and in terms of attitudes.

Accessibility is being addressed head on in some areas of the UK, particularly in relation to availability of accessible changing places for people with profound and multiple learning disabilities. The PAMIS (Promoting a More Inclusive Society) Changing Places campaign (see Appendix 11) is beginning to have an impact. The box below describes some of the developments that we found, and how they were achieved. This is exciting progress. Many services, however, have yet to find creative ways forward in their own local area, and 'lack of community changing facilities' was commonly mentioned as an issue.

Accessible changing places in Nottingham

The day service modernisation manager in Nottingham used the PAMIS Changing Places campaign video to help persuade neighbourhood services, chief officers and councillors that work was needed to achieve accessible facilities locally. A working group of Access officers, architects, occupational therapists, physiotherapists and staff from neighbourhood services created a design and then tried it out using a 'mock-up'. The council has been convinced: the redevelopment of the Market Square in Nottingham will include an adult changing facility, and others are in the pipeline too.

Area 4 (North Lanarkshire)

Community centres in Shotts and Moodiesburn have been refurbished to provide better access for disabled people. New changing areas have been developed with tracking and hoist equipment. The initiative, achieved through the day service modernisation strategy, received a Corporate Award in the category of promoting social inclusion.

The role of health staff in supporting people to use ordinary community facilities is quite striking. We found several examples of health-funded projects and initiatives, often linked to health promotion activities, that are supporting people to go out and about in community places. What they offer is purposeful, and it is also fun. Some examples are shown below.

Promoting health through cycling

Pedal Power in Cardiff arose from the work of physiotherapists and has developed into a separate charity. It is run by volunteers with advice from a sessional cycling coach, and has its own adapted cycles. It's currently based in a caravan park with access to traffic free parkland and the Taff Trail. People cycle for up to an hour, for exercise, to try cycling out, or just for fun.

Promoting mental health
The **Body Balance Group**, at the South West Yorkshire Mental Health Trust, provides individual and group exercise sessions to improve people's fitness and health and, through that, their mental health. They use ordinary settings, like the local gym. Some people have gone on to use the gym on their own.

Many people we met talked about the importance of having 'local' options. At strategic level, 'going local' underpins many of the ways services are developing. In Area 4, where day centres have been replaced by 'locality services', the strategy is to recruit local people. If a support worker actually lives in the area, then they are likely to know what is going on and how to access it. In rural areas going local helps to address travelling issues and to connect people with the community in which they live, as developments in Shropshire have demonstrated.

The move towards community-based services is delivering more local opportunities for many people. There is evidence that services are more systematically mapping where people live and the facilities and groups that are out there in local communities for people to access and link with. Pure Innovations in Stockport, for example, has set up teams that focus on local community issues, such as dealing with litter and working with the local council. There are also services being set up with a clear 'sign-posting' role, linking people into those mainstream opportunities and diverting them away from entering the world of day services. We heard of both transition and advocacy projects that are fulfilling this role, but also met families who are 'doing it themselves'. One set of parents had found both work placements their son had during his transition period at school (in the local post office and in the library). As they said, 'It's being local and being seen by your neighbours. That's very important to most parents.'

In settings specific to their cultural preferences

A survey of families from Asian communities in Bradford found they liked individual support, someone from their own community who could 'hold their hand' and help them to access services.[98] The importance of this key worker model is well established in the literature[93] and was reflected in what we found in practice. Some services that have been specifically designed to build the trust of families from black and minority ethnic groups were found to be successfully supporting people to go out from the family home to do things. Most of these 'day opportunities' have been developed by ethnic advocacy services responding to an identified need, and are located in areas with a high level of diversity in the local population. Such projects do not, however, appear to be widespread.

> **The Ethnic Minority Access and Participation Project (EMAPP) in Hounslow and Ealing**
> EMAPP provides information, advice and general advocacy to family carers of people from minority ethnic groups – but it does much more than that! The project has started a single sex group for Asian women with learning disabilities that meets in a community building, and has just started a similar group at weekends. Both are badged as 'respite' services but their aim is to empower and support people to do community-based activities.

Overall we struggled to locate specific initiatives for people from black and minority ethnic communities. We heard of just one commissioned, standalone service with a specific remit to provide day opportunities for people from black and minority ethnic communities (see 'Holy Bones' on page 58). A few day services have specific workers for people from black and minority ethnic groups, and we located two targeted services for Asian women that are run by larger day services. Such initiatives are essential, especially for women from communities where same-sex environments and support are required outside of the home.

> **The day service for Asian women in Waltham Forest**
> The service supports 16 women who enjoy a range of community-based activities using (mainly) community facilities around the borough. Some also attend an advocacy group for black and asian women run by Powerhouse in Newham. Twelve women attend mainstream adult education classes, and three

are supported in work experience. As part of their commitment to families the team agrees not to leave a woman alone in the company of men if that's what the family requires. The service has been successful because it works closely with families.

The Roshni day service for Asian women at Options for Life in Sandwell
The service was set up about nine years ago in response to local need, and supports around 13 women. Building the trust of family carers is an important element of their work with the women and their families. The aim is to support the women to lead a full life in the community, with activities that include Asian cooking and English as a second language.

We have not been able to establish what impact such targeted services for people from black and minority ethnic minority groups are having on larger-scale day and employment services or to what extent direct payments are being used as another route to appropriate support. This is an important area for further research.

There are things that *all* services can do, as is illustrated below.

In Area 6 (Pure Innovations), a single network operates for people from black and minority ethnic communities and for disabled people. Their literature naturally includes black people with learning disabilities who have gained jobs through supported employment, and some who have won awards for their achievements. It helps to convey that the service is open to *all*.

3.7.3 *Why* people are doing things

Based on their own desires and aspirations

Are people doing things that they really want to do and that are right for them? Are they being supported to achieve their personal goals and ambitions?

It is a very mixed picture. All the supported employment services contacted are using individual profiling approaches to guide their work with individuals. Looking more widely across *all* community-based services there is clearly a push to deliver services in more person-centred ways. People are certainly 'talking the talk' of person-centredness. In the larger community-based day services, however, there is still a sense of people responding to an offer, rather than the offer responding to what a person wants. This is also true of FE opportunities and was a source of frustration for several managers.

In practice, we found person-centred planning to be more evident in small, voluntary sector services and projects, and that overall it is not yet having a major effect on the lives of most people with a learning disability.

A number of transition projects contacted during the survey are carrying out person-centred planning with young people with learning disabilities. Invariably, it is an approach that moves outside traditional 'service' areas, and encourages someone to consider their whole life, who they want to be, and where they want to go in life.

'What the young person is saying they want, that is the starting point. That gives them a sense of autonomy, if they are saying they want something and they see it happening. But if they don't like it in the end, then we try to unpick that – if it is to do with someone they went with, or whether it is the occupation. Then they have knowledge as well, of what they like and don't like.'
(manager, Area 3, Promoting Independence Project)

In each of the transition projects people's families and natural friendship circles were included in their planning in order to maximise their own leadership and involvement. Some planning had been led by family members.

Mary was isolated and depressed, and stayed at home most of the time. The person-centred planning coordinator visited her and got to know her and her family. One weekend all the people who knew Mary well gathered together and the coordinator went to the home, equipped with a large sheet of paper and

> pens. In one afternoon they helped Mary identify her goals and dreams. She wanted to be outdoors, and loved gardening. As the coordinator explained: ... that is why we started the allotment, so she would have somewhere to go to do something she liked doing. And then we discovered that a couple of other young people liked to do gardening, so they were offered the opportunity to go to the allotment If they didn't like it – they wouldn't need to go again. So, that development came out of an individual's wishes.'

Individualisation does not mean that people need to be isolated when doing things during the day, as we can see from Mary's example above. However, service models that are based on group or 'block' funding ultimately constrain individual choice. In areas that have tried to individualise budgets or are using direct payments it appears to be much simpler, as one service manager explained:

> 'The PCP (person-centred planning) drives everything. If someone moves from one provider to another, they won't lose their PCP, or their house.'

Many tools for person-centred planning naturally help to address people's communication needs. In Area 7 (London Borough of Newham, NuLife Day and Employment Opportunities) videos and multi-media are also being used so that people can understand and relate to their own plan. Multi-media support has been deliberately commissioned as part of a strategy to involve people fully in their planning.

In Area 4 the local authority and every service provider delivers training in person-centred approaches to planning. All of the 300+ service users have a plan and an implementation specification.

Staff need to be committed to listening to people and able to think creatively to make plans happen. We heard many creative approaches.

> Alan, who has significant impairments, enjoys being around cars. He wanted to get work in a garage, but the job coach could not find a garage that would employ him. She worked out a

plan with Alan to start up a micro-enterprise and become self-employed. With a bank loan he bought himself a power hose, and rents a space from a supported living organisation to keep his paperwork. He now enjoys running his own business and, as he says "I am happy and proud when I see a clean car, and when the customer pays me".

What people do gives shape to their lives, makes sense for them; it's meaningful and purposeful

'I think my life has been very much improved lately, in the past couple of years. Kept on growing and growing.'

(person with learning disabilities)

Community-based day and employment services appear to be supporting people, in general, to do things that are more purposeful than in previous service models.

However, organisational issues in statutory services act as a barrier to delivering services that really do make sense for each individual, particularly the numbers of people who require support set against the resources they have to provide it. This is explored further in Section 4. In Stockport, statutory day services have moved out of the local authority and formed a not-for-profit organisation. It has opened up possibilities that have enabled services to grow and change, and become more person-centred.

Since moving from the local authority in 2005, with agreement from social services, **Pure Innovations** (Area 6) has been eligible for funding not available to local authorities. The service currently runs a museum, a community radio station, cafes in several local museums and historic houses and a high street cafe. People are working alongside park wardens to maintain and upgrade local parks. One day centre currently remains and is gradually supporting people to find new opportunities. Employment and volunteering are the core elements of the organisation. Self- advocates and parents are important players in its management.

Direct payments enable people to choose pursuits that make sense and have meaning for them. As one parent said:

'We use a direct payment which gives us heaps of choice and opportunity to be included in what is out there already'.

But when the person has profound and multiple learning disabilities 'what is out there' may be quite limited. With colleges generally not serving people with higher needs, employment schemes largely focusing on people whose support can be faded, and few social firms offering opportunities for people with higher needs the remaining options seem to be focused on home, leisure and personal health.

People often take up an activity because they are motivated to earn money and to make a contribution to society.

In Area 4 (North Lanarkshire), both the people we interviewed who were working in cafes, and one person working on the tills in a supermarket found their jobs tiring. It was often an effort to keep up the work. However, they stuck at it because it earned them money, and they could then relax and enjoy their leisure time more. In one case the young woman was using her earnings to fund driving lessons, and she was also able to enjoy an active social life with her friends.

We heard about other incentives being used to help people stay motivated, both as employees (for example, an employee of the month award) and as recipients of day service support (for example, achievement certificates). These have been well received and valued by people with learning disabilities. They help give meaning and purpose to people's efforts.

3.7.4 *How* people are doing things

People make choices and decisions, and fully participate in doing things

A person-centred approach looks beyond the 'service offer' and encourages someone to think first about his or her own goals. However, options need to be explained clearly in order for people to make genuine choices. In several services, and particularly within employment projects, a menu approach was in evidence. People could experience a range of options, often in the form of work tasters or short work placements.

> In Area 2 (The orchardville Society) young people aged 16-19 are regularly offered three work placements while still at school. This enables them to make an informed choice. One parent explained the advantages of this system: '... he could make up his mind at age 19 – 'what is it you want to do?'. He found the office totally boring and didn't want to work there, and he chose the coffee shop'. The parent had actually preferred the 'set up' in the office work, but she accepted his choice since he had tried the alternatives.

To be active in the community people need good information about what's on offer and what's happening. We have discussed community mapping on page 89. Much of this work is being led by self-advocacy groups or staff in 'community builder' or inclusion-focused roles. People with learning disabilities are very involved, and some are paid.

Participating and doing things for yourself means learning and developing skills. We found a focus on systematic and structured learning particularly in projects working with younger people and in supported employment, less in the general community-based day services. Greater access to information about structured approaches may be helpful for staff.

As more people with learning disabilities succeed in real jobs, their stories can and will inspire others.[1] We heard from several services about DVDs and videos that had been produced to spread the word through people telling their own stories to others.

> In Area 1 (Brandon Trust), people were asking to train and work in parks. As the service manager explained: 'our learners were very much saying that what they wanted was to do what the parks department do'. But there wasn't an amenity horticultural qualification. A local park was wanting more community

support so the service teamed up with the college to access LSC funding for a parks-based training project. As the manager said, the project ticked all the boxes: '1 that it was able to be funded by education, 2 that it met the needs of our learners in terms of what they were telling us, and 3 that it gave us lots of opportunities to link up with other partners, but also be very prevalent in that community'. The project is now in its second year, and the team are developing a new qualification that will be accredited through the FE college.

With the right amount and type of support needed ... to be as independent as possible

Overall it is probably the relationship between the person and their support worker that makes the greatest impact. We heard several examples of people who are receiving individualised support being involved in interviewing and choosing their own support staff. This potentially switches the locus of control from staff to the person with learning disabilities.

In more group-focused services, however, that shift in power between service user and supporter was not fully observed. Staff training is vital: a good basic offer for support staff would include disability equality training, person-centred planning and approaches and communication training. There was widespread evidence of staff accessing basic introductory training around person-centred approaches. There was less evidence that services are systematically supporting people to maximise their communication, although there are pockets of good practice.

Hackney Independent Living Team (HILT)

HILT's day service team moved away from a buildings base a few years ago. The team supports several people with quite complex needs, including people with autism, so the organisation invested in multi-media training and support through Acting Up (see Appendix 11), and in specific skills training. People supported by the team now have visual diaries and prompts, and staff use more structured approaches. People who have been excluded by other services are using community facilities and public transport with very individualised support.

Services supporting people in their own tenancies are increasingly being expected to take over support during the day as part of day service modernisation strategies, a push that's modelled on the success of organisations like **Inclusion Glasgow** and **The Ling Trust**. This push towards achieving an integrated whole life approach for more people will only be successful, however, if it is backed up by commissioning strategies that ensure services have adequate resources to provide support during the day, staff themselves receive development and support, and there are effective monitoring systems in place. It is possible that it will only *remain* successful if organisations stay small and very focused. **Partners for Inclusion** in Ayrshire delivers individualised, person-centred approaches that support people to do the things they want to do directly from home. It originally grew out of Inclusion Glasgow, and the organisations now work closely together, sharing learning and supporting each other. In Area 7 a local independent sector provider, Heritage Care, re-organised its **New Avenues** day service so that staff now support people directly from home rather than from a day centre. An account of their journey and the steps they took can be found in Cole and Lloyd.[95]

During the survey we met people with significant needs who have 24-hour individual support. Personal support workers or assistants can really get to know an individual, and can also provide a valuable link into community resources.

A young man we met in Area 4 had recently finished his college course and just moved into his own house. That was the main thing he wanted to talk about. As he said: 'I like it, because I've got a front and back door. I chose that.' Like any young person, he wants to take his time developing outside interests and a possible career. He is having some 'gap' time to settle in and feel his feet. He has a team of support workers who understand this, but at the same time they are helping him to think about what he could do during the day. There is now a list of places he likes to go to on his fridge that he can refer to if he feels bored – mainly leisure activities, including football, bowling and other sports. He told us that he will think about a career in the future.

In Area 5 (Thurrock) the role of personal assistant has been created within the community day service to work with some people who have the highest support needs. They are trying to manage their resources to focus support according to need.

For people with profound and multiple learning disabilities the level of support needed to access community facilities has in the past proved a challenge that services have found hard to meet. With some services developing new purpose-built provision there is a real danger that those services will again find it difficult to support people to access facilities and opportunities outside of the building. It is yet to be seen whether such provision can accurately be called a community base, or whether in reality, they will simply be smaller, relocated day centres.

Because people with high support needs are relatively 'high cost' users of community care resources the funding of individualised support through direct and indirect payments can become a cost-neutral option, especially if ILF monies are accessed. To achieve more individualised support for more people, however, will inevitably require money to be freed up from exisitng *services*, but as managers repeatedly commented:

> '… as yet we have not been able to unlock the money tied up in large day services.'

Above all, people with profound and complex needs should be at the head of the queue for person-centred planning and individualised support packages. It makes a real difference.

Sally was excluded from her special school because of 'challenging behaviour'. Her mum didn't want her going to a day centre so she hired a tutor with her own money to teach Sally at home. The tutor focused on teaching Sally to communicate using pictures, about 'home' responsibilities and personal care. With some help Sally's mum developed a support plan for Sally to continue living at home in her community. Now Sally, with her mum's help, gets direct payments and ILF to hire the support Sally needs to continue her learning. She goes out in the community shopping, walking her dog, to music classes and swimming. Sally can now use pictures fluently to communicate as well as some speech. Her mum says 'she is a totally different Sally'.

The *amount* of support that people require may to some extent be determined by whether they live with their families; the role of day services and employment in giving carers a break is important to consider. It appears that voluntary and independent sector services that have been developed anew are providing people with a low number of hours of support each week relative to that provided to people in services 'modernised' from day centres. Many people continue to rely on the modernised services for the bulk of their weekly support, and carers continue to rely on them for a break. They continue to act as the 'contingency' for people trying new options, such as employment. These factors all create constraints and challenges for those services and, in the absence of additional resources, impact on their ability to provide truly person-centred, flexible and responsive support.

Some services, however, are finding ways forward. In **Windsor** a partnership with a local girls school, linked to the personal social and health education (PHSE) national curriculum, led to a buddy scheme that has opened up community-based social activities for people in the evenings. Some services are deliberately using agency staff to create flexibility, or actively managing staff hours to cover longer days. In some instances it is simply active management or a more strategic approach that is needed to maximise the support and opportunities available to people.

3.8 Service delivery, management and strategic issues in community-based support

The design, development and delivery of the services we heard about have been influenced by a number of different factors.

3.8.1 Parents

The influence of parents was often described as negative in terms of blocking planned initiatives, yet there is evidence that some parents and families have had a very positive impact in organising direct payments and individualised support for their sons and daughters. Some good services have grown from parental pressure and action. It's a very mixed picture, but the common thread is that people *are* very aware of the need to engage with and involve families, and there are emerging structures and approaches that give families an *ongoing* voice in developments.

3.8.2 The voice of people with learning disabilities

For people with learning disabilities the picture is encouraging in the number of initiatives we found that have grown out of and are being led by self-advocacy groups, albeit mainly leisure and information focused. Of concern, however, is that very few areas appear to be regularly collating information from people's individual and person-centred plans about what they want and what's happening for them, and using the findings *in a strategic way* to influence and shape their ongoing developments.[95]

> 'Shaping the Future Together', a structured approach that aggregates information from individual planning for strategic planning purpose, was piloted in Area 5. It showed that a significant number of people using day services still wanted to work. As well as following each the individuals, the information gathered was used as evidence for funding bids to extend employment support, two of which were successful.

3.8.3 National and local policies and the effect of externalisation

In general, national policies are being used as a positive and helpful force for change, but local policies and priorities get mixed press from commissioners and managers trying to achieve community-based day and employment support.

The prevailing political ethos in a local area has undoubtedly had an impact, particularly in relation to 'externalisation', moving existing services out of the local authority. Since moving out, with the blessing of the local authority, Pure Innovations in Stockport has flourished. The majority of the employment initiatives surveyed are in the voluntary sector, many originating from the local authority. This positioning enables them to access more funding streams, and many now have multiple and complex funding sources. Arguably, it may also suggest that employment support is not seen as core local authority business. Almost all the employment initiatives contacted commented on the amount of time spent preparing funding bids, and their lack of a permanent financial footing. For some this has threatened their existence. 'Externalising' services and developing voluntary and independent sector services brings opportunities, but without support (in whatever form) they may not survive. We heard of some valued, community-based initiatives that no longer exist.

3.8.4 A strategic and systemic approach

National policies have pushed local areas to be more strategic in their approach to day service modernisation and developing employment. This has been welcomed. Many of the voluntary sector services we talked to did not, however, know if, or how they linked into their local strategy. Some felt that they could be of benefit to people using local authority day services and thereby day service modernisation plans, but it simply wasn't happening. It appears that in many areas developments are still not 'joined up' across providers.

> Area 4 has a very joined-up strategy, extremely person-centred, and based on clear values that people are individuals and have a right to be in the community and using ordinary community supports. Its strongest points are its connectedness, the sense of values reflected by people we met at every level, and the fact that we met people who have a life....

Strategic commissioning is greatly aided by good information, especially about quality and costs of different services. The majority of services could provide information about budgets, but not about how much the service was costing for individuals. With the development of self-directed services and increased use of direct payments support services will need to be able to provide indicative individualised costings. This is an urgent developmental need.

The relationship between the work of supported employment services and the role of staff in other community day services has been, and in many areas, remains unclear. In some a clearer role is developing for day service staff around work preparation and volunteering; elsewhere we found community day service staff taking on job seeking and job coaching. Whatever strategy is adopted needs to be a clear one that is backed by appropriate training for staff.

Removing the division between residential and day supports helps people to have a more 'whole life' *if and when* person-centred planning underpins the support. We have heard about the positive changes that have resulted for people supported by such services. Strategically, service providers with such a clear value base and approach are relatively rare and may need to be 'grown' in local areas.

3.8.5 Leadership and service culture

The most important anchor point must be the values and philosophy on which services are based. In Area 4 all staff are offered underpinning values training that emphasises applying the same standards to the lives of people we support as we do to our own. The lead commissioner said that it was often very challenging for staff to start thinking in this way. We heard that at least some staff in most of the services contacted have received training in person-centred approaches. We also found several services where people with learning disabilities are providing training to staff in a range of settings, including the Police, libraries and museums.

Commissioners and managers have an important role to play in shaping people's thinking and approaches, modelling respect and value for others and emphasising the 'ordinary'. Where change has been wide-scale, there is often a key individual who has driven developments forward over a sustained period of time. The way commissioners and, especially, managers operate influences the culture of a service. We met several managers who emphasised the need to 'think like a business', and not just in employment services. People are aware that they are operating in a different arena that requires partnerships with a wide range of community bodies in order to achieve the opportunities and support that people want.

Strong leadership can be about planning ahead, freeing up money, finding ways of offering choices, problem solving. It is about taking people with you, and we met several people in new and modernised services with those qualities. Several people specifically mentioned when they had a good local leader, and clearly valued it. Leadership is also about seeing opportunities and building something from them. Some of the best initiatives we have heard about have grown in just that way. The **Garstang Deanery Project** (see page 84), for example, grew out of a chance meeting between the local authority commissioner and the Canon of the Deanery at a social event.

But leadership can come from others too, as the manager stressed below.

> 'We think good sustainable solutions are more likely to come from the 'bottom-up' rather than by being imposed from above. We would rather let people 'own' things.'

We have demonstrated how leadership from people with learning disabilities and families is having an impact, but it remains on the fringe at the moment and much more could be happening. We are not sure if this is about the will to do it, or practicalities around support.

We heard evidence that people at *all* levels are taking initiative and working creatively. It is what is required in community settings, but people have stressed that the supportive infrastructure needs to be there too.

3.8.6 Resources

The availability of capital money (whether new allocation or released from the sale of day centres) has had an impact on the shape of developments. How the capital money has been used reflects the creativity of local commissioners and planners. Many have used it to develop new community bases, often in partnership with others (see page 84).

Having an existing day centre building can be an asset where it is used strategically to pump-prime community development.

In **Southampton** the money released from the sale of a day centre is being combined with a grant from Sport England to refurbish and expand a community centre as a community sports resource. The new centre will be managed by local residents including people with learning disabilities. It is part of a day service modernisation strategy that will re-invest capital money from day centre sales into the development of

> three community facilities for the benefit of all members of the community.

It is encouraging to see capital money also being used to develop accessible changing facilities in community places, as in Shropshire and Nottingham, and to invest in multi-media training and equipment in Newham. Residual revenue funding from hospital closure has been used in Norfolk to create a base-less service for people with higher support needs.

The day service modernisation sites we talked to, however, have mainly achieved their move to a community-based service with no extra revenue funding. As described by one manager, changes had to be 'cost neutral'. This has undoubtedly been a significant factor in how their developments have shaped up. How services have used the existing revenue, tied up in staffing, building maintenance and operational costs, has been key. Overall, the move appears to be to rental or leasing of community bases rather than ownership. Few areas are developing base-less services. Some areas have transferred a portion of the revenue or staff from 'old' day services into employment services to extend capacity.

Of particular concern are the number of new initiatives that have been set up with short-term funding. Some of the most person-centred practices were found in small voluntary sector projects with just one, two or three years' funding. Many expressed serious concerns about their sustainability. Such uncertainty about the future does not help services to thrive.

Community care purchasing budgets are under pressure. For direct payments and individualised funding to grow money has to be released from the block funding of day services. It's a complex challenge that has to be faced, and it has to be faced soon given the development of self-directed services. Managers of day services across *all* sectors will need help to identify the implications for their service and make the necessary preparations and adjustments to the way they operate.

3.8.7 Partnership approaches

Developing community-based support and social inclusion services means developing a far greater range of partners – community partners. It is about working with local councillors and the council strategy for all its citizens; developing partnerships with businesses, other providers, churches and faith groups, pressure groups, public facilities, transport services, housing providers and planners. It is about networks, cooperatives, action groups, advisory groups, learning from each other, trusting, negotiating, giving....

We have illustrated, in the box below and throughout the report, some of the innovative partnership work we have found, and the benefits that have resulted.

Productive partnerships

The Garstang Deanery Project, near Blackburn
The project is a partnership between the Blackburn diocese and local authority social services that focuses on social inclusion and aims to build natural supports and divert people from using day services. Money from a day centre post has been transferred to the project to make it happen.

In Chester, Ellesmere Port and Neston
Partnership working between a local health promotion practitioner and the Borough Council's active communities officer has paid dividends. With sports development funding a low impact aerobic group for people with learning disabilities was started in the evening at a local leisure centre. There are now two running in different centres. They have been taken over by the leisure centres and are on the mainstream activities list. People pay at the door like anyone else.

In Cheshire
150 work experience opportunities have been developed for young people in transition through a partnership between the LSC, Connexions, West Cheshire FE College, Scope, Cheshire

county council and Education Business Partnership. The Supported Employment Scheme also runs a 'Positive Awards for Business' annual awards ceremony that celebrates the contribution of employers in the recruitment, employment and opportunities offered to disabled people.

In Poole
A formal partnership has been developed between the Borough of Poole's adult services and the local jobcentre. Two staff from the Supported Employment team are now based at the jobcentre alongside other mainstream employment staff.

3.8.8 Workforce policies and approaches

Roles and responsibilities for support staff are developing and changing! We heard about community development workers, leisure and sports co-ordinators, community bridge-builders, personal assistants, job coaches, employment advisers, circles facilitators, buddies and more.

In Somerset
A national pilot project[109] has been investigating a new role of community enabler. Focusing on developing support within a local community, two separate cafes have evolved organically and become local community-based facilities. A range of people have used the cafes, including older people, people with learning disabilities, physical disabilities and mental health issues. Members of the public have also joined sessions from word of mouth, and enjoyed sharing skills or time with people there.

We also, however, saw that many staff who are supporting people in community settings are still working to old day service contracts and job descriptions. Flexible working times are being achieved through their goodwill and with good management of staff team hours. Having job descriptions and contracts that support the work people are expected to do helps, but people stressed that it is about more than that. One voluntary sector manager pointed out that it really helps to:

> '… employ staff who are confident all round communicators, good at asking, good at spotting opportunities, good at organising themselves and their work, who are goal driven and don't come with preconceptions about what people can do.'

We did not see staff job descriptions or contracts as part of this survey, so cannot comment on how they are changing to support new approaches and community ways of working. It is likely that some of the more innovative services have workforce policies and systems that would be of interest and help to managers who are shaping community support services now.

Recruiting and retaining staff is an issue for some services. Agency staff are being used for cover, and as a deliberate strategy at times to reduce expenditure. Further work is needed to establish the impact that this has on the quality of support that people receive.

Clear direction and leadership, a supervision structure, enabling systems and good partnerships are important to providing a committed body of staff who will have the flexibility to support people in new and person-centred ways.

In Area 5, job descriptions for staff in day centres were changed to create a personal assistant role for people with high support needs. Other staff moved to become 'community facilitators' and 'community workers', undertaking community mapping as part of their role.

We found two areas where transfer of undertakings for public employees arrangements have been used to transfer staff from local authority day services into external organisations. In Bromley the local authority has developed a contract with the **Shaw Trust** to develop social firms. Staff have transferred to support people working in Tuck by Truck, a catering enterprise, and on a cemetery maintenance contract, with more firms developing.

Whoever employs staff it is important that they have well thought-out strategies to achieve community integration in practice. We found some evidence of a strategic approach at practice level, particularly in supported employment schemes, but overall it appears that trial and error rules.

'We try not to be involved in anything which is segregated. If somebody wanted to learn to tap dance, we wouldn't set up a tap dancing group. We would look for a tap dancing group in the community, which that one person could join.'

3.8.9 Minimising risk

Quality services care about people and about what happens to them, and because of this they have effective systems in place to ensure that people are getting good support and a good service. Good support is a big concern for parents. Many want to know that there are good systems in place to minimise and manage risks when people are using community facilities and settings. They want to know that someone is monitoring what is going on when a worker is supporting an individual 'out there'.

There are many strategies being used to manage and minimise risks, including use of mobile 'phones, people carrying personal information, detailed vocational profiling and job matching, supported 'tasters', risk assessments on community settings and support fading techniques. It was not mentioned as a significant issue by services. Services supporting people who present challenges, where issues of risk may have been anticipated, have commented that people's behaviours have changed and the risks have naturally reduced. There is some evidence, however, that this may be being achieved through increasing a person's support rather than planned strategies and managed interventions.

Monitoring systems are crucial to ensure that people are receiving the right amount and type of support they need when they are 'out and about' in community settings. Ensuring quality is one step towards addressing family concerns about community-based provision, but managing the quality of community-based support is different than managing the quality of service delivery within a building.

The **Community Day Services Team** in Waltham Forest, East London, has built regular practice monitoring, including spot checks, into its structure. One day service officer and a manager are 'on duty' each day. Being 'on duty' includes monitoring visits to people while they are being supported out and around the borough. The checks and findings are recorded centrally on a database that is accessible to all managers. Actions are taken to address any concerns. It is a systematic approach.

We heard little mention or detail of ongoing practice-monitoring strategies, although there *was* evidence of services undertaking annual reviews and evaluations and gathering feedback from people with learning disabilities and families as part of that process. Many of the supported employment services had good systems to track progress and achievements, and had been evaluated by external agencies. We remain concerned that many services appear to need a more systematic approach to monitoring day-to-day practice.

3.8.10 'Situational' factors

Without a doubt the shape of new developments has been influenced by geographical location, particularly whether it is a rural or urban area, but also the type of area in terms of its economic and social opportunities. For example, the development of an integrated whole life approach may be dependent to some extent on features of the local housing market; staff recruitment and retention may be affected by cost of living, availability of affordable accommodation, availability of regeneration-type funding and other local employment opportunities. There is no 'one way' – developments have to fit the local area.

They also have to fit the demographics of the local population and levels of need, current and projected. Concerns were expressed during the survey that community-based services, particularly employment-focused, are reaching capacity. More planning with an eye to future demand is needed.

3.9 Conclusions

Community-based day and employment support is very diverse and still developing. There is no single model that is 'right' and people in all parts of the UK are grappling daily with different challenges that are often unique to their area and service context. Notwithstanding, there are some important themes and messages that emerge from this practice survey.

In terms of establishing employment for people, it helps to:

- shift resources from day services into employment support. The greater the number of employment advisers and job coaches the higher the number of people supported into paid work each year
- listen carefully to what people want to do. Some may not want paid work, and may be better placed as volunteers, needing a service that is outside the 'supported employment' model. This is a role that modernised day services could fulfill
- ensure that work tasters or placements are strictly about experience or training and are time-limited, with help built in so that people move on into genuine paid work. Expect that people can, and should work. Start early with offer work tasters to young people
- use stories of people's success in work to encourage employers, people with learning disabilities, family carers and others
- work with jobcentres so they increase their focus on people with learning disabilities
- develop care managers, social workers and day service staff so that they more actively and positively shape people's expectations about work.

In moving towards community-based services, it helps to:

- create local solutions
- nurture the support of family networks, friends and relations through good involvement and partnership strategies, and evidence of reliable, safe community-based practice
- develop deliberate practice strategies to build connections and inclusion, and thereby develop natural supports around people
- take things one step at a time and celebrate success so that others can see it is possible
- prioritise people with higher support needs to ensure they have the opportunity for individualised support and can take up opportunities in community settings
- work with people from black and minority ethnic communities to create solutions they see as acceptable

- develop wide partnerships to build a welcoming community infra-structure
- use capital money creatively, and not to create buildings 'for the service'
- invest in local leaders and champions
- create new job roles and responsibilities, and flexible working hours
- keep as much money as possible flexible and available for support – not tied up in running buildings.

To ensure that people are doing what they want to do, it helps to:

- make sure that person-centred approaches are in place
- plan with younger people, in particular, in a person-centred way. Their families can then be involved in a natural way to help lead the plan
- individualise funding: attach it to each person, especially people who need higher levels of support so that community inclusion happens for them
- recruit, develop and support staff to be creative and lateral thinking, and to keep finding solutions as people change and develop their aspirations
- make sure people get good information about choices, including stories from people who have pursued their own wishes and dreams and succeeded.

3.9.1 Next steps

This practice survey has focused on best of practice in different parts of the UK. However, there are still gaps in the available information about current practice that this project has not been able to fill. These include the following:

- information about college and continuing education provision for adults with learning disabilities, and the role it plays in their lives. This should include information from the LSC pathfinder projects
- the costs of service provision at an individual level

- evaluative information that will reveal and compare quality in different service models. There is a tendency to 'showcase' good practice, and not to examine and monitor what is going on
- information about the daytime lives of people in more complex situations, such as people with high support needs, or people who present challenges in relation to community-based day opportunities
- The impact that targeted services for people from black and minority ethnic groups are having on larger-scale day and employment services, and the extent to which direct payments are being used as a route to culturally appropriate support
- strategies for moving social firms onto a business footing
- effective models and strategies for recruiting, training and developing staff into new roles
- whether the 'clubhouse' model really is shifting power and control into the hands of people with learning disabilities, and deserves further exploration.

There are also a number of areas of practice that could be strengthened through provision of information and practice guidance:

For commissioners, managers and care managers around:

- costing services
- monitoring of community-based service delivery
- lessons from LSC pathfinder projects
- effective, person-centred transition planning
- how to release money from the block funding of day services.

For local politicians and Board members around:

- policy and best practice in day service modernisation
- funding strategies for sustainability.

For staff in community-based day services around:

- Training in Systematic Instruction
- work preparation, including developing self-employment

- strategies for achieving inclusion and building community connections.

For managers and staff in social firms and sheltered workshops around:

- how to moving on to a business footing
- self-employment (micro-enterprise).

All these areas require further research, evaluation or development effort, and some require a more in-depth approach. This practice survey and the research review it accompanies have highlighted the fact that practice is often outstripping the published literature. People with learning disabilities, their families, supporters and managers all need more clarity about how to proceed. Our experience from this survey indicates that guidance will be welcomed, and will help people with learning disabilities to 'have a good day'.

References

1   Simons, K. and Watson, D. (1999) *New directions: Day services for people with learning disabilities in the 1990s: A review of the research*, Bristol: Norah Fry Research Centre, University of Bristol.

2   Ward, L. (2000) 'Learning difficulties', *Research Matters*, No 8, October 1999/April 2000, pp 62–64.

3   Emerson, E., Malam, S., Davies, I. and Spencer, K. (2005) *Adults with learning difficulties in England 2003/04*, London: Health and Social Care Information Centre.

4   McIntosh, B. (1998) 'Better days ahead', *Care Plan*, vol 4, no 4, pp 8–12.

5   Perrins, K. and Tarr, J. (1998) 'The quality of day care provision to encourage the transition to adulthood for young women with learning difficulties', *Research in Post-Compulsory Education*, vol 3, no 1, p 93–109.

6   Veck, W. (2002) 'Completing the story: connecting relational and psychological process of exclusion', *Disability and Society*, vol 17, no 5, pp 529–540.

7   Beyer, S., Grove, B., Schneider, J., Simons, K., Williams, V., Heyman, A., Swift, P. and Krijnen-Kemp, E. (2004) *Working lives: The role of day centres in supporting people with learning disabilities into employment*, DWP Research Report 203, Leeds: Corporate Document Services.

8   Department of Health (2003) *Fulfilling lives: Inspection of services for people with learning disabilities*, London: DH.

9   Jahoda, A. and Markova, I. (2004) 'Coping with social stigma: people with intellectual disabilities moving from institutions and family home', *Journal of Intellectual Disability Research*, vol 48, no 8, pp 719–729.

10 Mencap (2002b) *Doing, showing and going: Mencap's arts strategy*, London: Mencap.

11 Hall, E. (2004) 'Social geographies of learning disability: narratives of exclusion and inclusion', *Area*, vol 36, no 3, pp 298–306.

12 Price, D. and Barron, L. (1999) 'Developing independence: the experience of the lawnmowers theatre company', *Disability and Society*, vol 14, no 6, pp 819–830.

13   Fursland, E. (2003) 'Stage coaches', *Community Care*, 1501: 40 (13 December).

14   Goodley, D. (2000) 'Acting out the individual programme plan: performance arts and innovative social policy for and by people with 'learning difficulties'', *Critical Social Policy*, vol 20, no 4, pp 503–532.

15   Bright, A. (2004) 'Power in the community: how community groups can achieve their goals' (available at www.elfrida.com/development.htm).

16   Cummins, R.A. and Lau, A.L.D. (2003) 'Community integration or community exposure? A review and discussion in relation to people with an intellectual disability', *Journal of Applied Research in Intellectual Disabilities*, vol 16, pp 145–157.

17   Williams, V. and Johnson, R. (2004) *Nice job if you can get it. Work and people with learning difficulties*, Ellesmere: Sequal trust.

18   Whitehouse, R., Chamberlain, P. and O'Brien, A. (2001) 'Increasing social interactions for people with more severe learning disabilities who have difficulty developing personal relationships', *Journal of Intellectual Disabilities*, vol 5, no 3, pp 209–220.

19   Forrester-Jones, R., Carpenter, J., Cambridge, P., Tate, A., Hallam, A., Knapp, M. and Beecham, J. (2002) 'The quality of life of people 12 years after resettlement from long stay hospitals: users' views on their living environment, daily activities and future aspirations', *Disability and Society*, vol 17, no 7, pp 741–758.

20   Dowson, S. (1998) *Certainties without centres: A discussion document on day services for people who have learning difficulties*, London: Values into Action.

21   Mencap (2002a) *A life in the day: The modernisation of day services for people with a learning disability*, London: Mencap.

22   Baker, P.A. (2000) 'Measurement of community participation and use of leisure by service users with intellectual disabilities: the Guernsey Community Participation and Leisure Assessment (GCPLA)', *Journal of Applied Research in Intellectual Disabilities*, vol 13, pp 169-185.

23   Srivastava, A. (2001) 'Developing friendships and social integration through leisure for people with moderate, severe and profound learning disabilities transferred from hospital to community care', *Tizard Learning Disability Review*, vol 6, no 4, pp 19–27.

24   Messent, P.R., Cooke, C.B. and Long, J. (2000) 'Secondary barriers to physical activity for adults with mild and moderate learning disabilities', *Journal of Intellectual Disabilities*, vol 4, no 3, pp 247–263.

25   Forrester-Jones, R. (2001) 'Developing friendships and social integration through leisure', *Tizard Learning Disability Review*, vol 6, no 4, pp 28–32.

26   Felce, D., Lowe, K., Perry, J., Jones, E., Baxter, H. and Bowley, C. (1999) 'The quality of residential and day services for adults with intellectual disabilities in eight local authorities in England: objective data gained in support of a social inspectorate inspection', *Journal of Applied Research in Intellectual Disabilities*, vol 12, no 4, pp 273–293.

27   Abraham, C., Gregory, N., Wolf, L. and Pemberton, R. (2002) 'Self-esteem, stigma and community participation among people with learning difficulties living in the community', *Journal of Community and Applied Social Psychology*, vol 12, no 6, pp 430-43.

28   Whittaker, A. and McIntosh, B. (2000) 'Changing days', *British Journal of Learning Disabilities*, vol 28, no 1, pp 3–8.

29   Pearson, C. (2000) 'Money talks? Competing discourses in the implementation of direct payments', *Critical Social Policy*, vol 20, no 4, pp 459–478.

30   Aspis, S. (2000) 'What users want', *Community Care*, 7 September.

31   Department of Health (1999) *Facing the facts: Services for people with learning disabilities: a policy impact study of social care and health services*, London: DH/SSI.

32   Scott, J. (2003) 'Benefit protection', *Community Care*, 11 September, pp 42–43.

33   Schneider, J., Simons, K. and Everatt, G. (2001) 'Impact of the national minimum wage on disabled people', *Disability and Society*, vol 16, no 5, pp 723–747.

34   Schneider, J. and Dutton, J. (2002) 'Attitudes towards disabled staff and the effect of the national minimum wage: a Delphi survey of employers and disability employment advisors', *Disability and Society*, vol 17, no 3, pp 283–306.

35 Elliott, C., Pring, T. and Bunning, K. (2002) 'Social skills training for adolescents with intellectual disabilities: a cautionary note', *Journal of Applied Research in Intellectual Disabilities*, vol 15, pp 91–96.

36 Harris, J. (2003) 'Time to make up your mind: why choosing is difficult', *British Journal of Learning Disabilities*, vol 31, no 1, pp 3–8.

37 Reynolds, F. (2002) 'An exploratory survey of opportunities and barriers to creative leisure activities for people with learning disabilities', *British Journal of Learning Disabilities*, vol 30, no 2, pp 63–67.

38 Beart, S., Hawkins, D., Stenfert-Kroese, B., Smithson, P. and Tolosa, I. (2001) 'Barriers to accessing leisure opportunities for people with learning difficulties', *British Journal of Learning Disabilities*, vol 29, pp 133–138.

39 Love., B., Bates, P. and Whitehead, S. (undated) *Valuing People Support Team* (undated), London: VPST.

40 Department of Health (1998) *Moving into the mainstream: The Report of a national audit of services for adults with learning disabilities*, London: DH/SSI.

41 Scottish Executive (2000) *The same as you? A review of services for people with learning disabilities*, Edinburgh: Scottish Executive.

42 Welsh Assembly (2001) *Fulfilling the promises*, Cardiff: Welsh Assembly.

43 Department of Health (2001) *Valuing People: A new strategy for learning disability for the 21st century*, Cmnd 5086, London: DH.

44 McIntosh, B. and Whittaker, A. (eds) (1998) *Days of change: A practical guide to developing better day opportunities with people with learning difficulties*, London: King's Fund.

45 Williams, V., Simons, K., Gramlich, S. McBride, G., Snelham, N. and Myers, B. (2003) 'Paying the piper and calling the tune: the relationship between parents and direct payments for people with intellectual disabilities', *Journal of Applied Research in Learning Disabilities*, vol 16, pp 219–228.

46 Short, A., Sanderson, H. and Cook, M. (2004) *Families leading planning: Looking to the future*, York: Helen Sanderson Associates.

47   Social Exclusion Unit (2005) *Improving services, improving lives: Evidence and key themes*, London: Office of the Deputy Prime Minister.

48   Department of Health (2005) *The story so far ... Statutory Instrument 2005 No 876 (C.37) The Carers (Equal Opportunities) Act 2004 (Commencement) (England) Order 2005*, London: DH.

49   Nissel, C. (1998) 'Thinking creatively on resettlement', *Care Plan*, vol 4, no 4, pp 17–19.

50   Robertson, J., Emerson, E., Hatton, C., Elliott, J., McIntosh, B., Swift, P., Krijnen-Kemp, E., Towers, C., Romeo, R., Knapp, M., Sanderson, H., Routledge, M., Oakes, P. and Joyce, T. (2005) *The impact of person centred planning*, Lancaster: University of Lancaster.

51   Flynn, M. (2005) *Developing the role of personal assistants*, Leeds: Skills for Care.

52   Holman, A. and Bewley, C. (1999) *Funding freedom 2000: People with learning difficulties using direct payments*, London: Values into Action.

53   Halliwell, S. and Glendinning, C. (1998) *Evaluation of the Manchester Direct Payments Scheme*, Manchester: National Primary Care Research and Development Centre, University of Manchester.

54   Stainton, T. and Boyce, S. (2004) '"I have got my life back": users' experience of direct payments', *Disability and society*, vol 19, no 4, pp 443–454.

55   Glendinning, C., Halliwell, S., Jacobs, S., Rummery, K. and Tyrer, J. (2000) *Buying independence: Using direct payments to integrate health and social services*, Bristol: The Policy Press.

56   Wilson, A., Riddell, S. and Baron, S. (2000) 'Welfare for those who can? The impact of the quasi-market on the lives of people with learning difficulties', *Critical Social Policy*, vol 20, no 4, pp 479–502.

57   Devas, M. (2003) 'Support and access in sports and leisure provision', *Disability and Society*, vol 18, no 2, pp 231–245.

58   Bates, P. and Davis, F.A. (2004) 'Social capital, social inclusion and services for people with learning disabilities', *Disability and Society*, vol 19, no 3, pp 195–207.

59   Wehmeyer, M.L. and Bolding, N. (2001) 'Enhanced self-determination of adults with intellectual disability as an outcome of moving to community-based work or living environments', *Journal of Intellectual Disability Research*, vol 45, no 5, pp 371–383.

60   Watson, D., Williams, V. and Wickham, C. (2005) *A valued part of the workforce? Employment and disabled people*, Guildford: The Sequal Development Partnership, University of Surrey.

61   Pannell, J., Simons, K. and Macadam, M. (2000) *Paid work and housing*, Brighton: Pavilion Publishing.

62   Williams, V. and Watson, D. (2001) *Behind the scenes: Work in Europe*, London: Mencap.

63   Ridley, J., Hunter, S. and Infusion Co-operative (2005) *Go for it! Supporting people with learning disabilities and/or autistic spectrum disorder in employment*, Edinburgh: Scottish Executive Social Research.

64   OSI (Open Society Institute) (2005) *Rights of people with intellectual disabilities: Access to education and employment*, Budapest: OSI.

65   Curry P. and Cupples, J. (2001) 'Ask the users', *Community Living*, vol 15, no 1, pp 18–20.

66   Gosling, V. and Cotterill, L. (2000) 'An employment project as a route to social inclusion for people with learning difficulties?', *Disability and Society*, vol 15, no 7, pp 1001–1018.

67   Secker, J., Dass, S. and Grove, B. (2003) 'Developing social firms in the UK: a contribution to identifying good practice,' *Disability and Society*, vol 18, no 5, pp 659–674.

68   Jones, S., Morgan, J., Murphy, D. and Shearn, J. (2002) *Making it work: Strategies for success in supported employment for people with learning difficulties*, Brighton: Pavilion Publishing.

69   Weston, J., Jones, C. and Stalker, K. (2002) *Supported employment for people with complex needs: Choosing, getting and keeping a job*, Edinburgh: Scottish Human Services Trust.

70   Shearn, J., Beyer, S. and Felce, D. (2000) 'The cost-effectiveness of supported employment for people with severe intellectual disabilities and high support needs: a pilot study', *Journal of Applied Research in Intellectual Disability*, vol 13, no 1, pp 29–37.

71   Forrester-Jones, R., Jones, S., Heason, S. and Di'Terlizzi, M. (2004) 'Supported employment: a route to social networks', *Journal of Applied Research in Intellectual Disabilities*, vol 17, pp 199–208.

72   Wilson, A. (2003) 'Real jobs, learning difficulties and supported employment', *Disability and Society*, vol 18, no 2, pp 99–115.

73   Stevens, P. and Martin, N. (1999) 'Supporting individuals with intellectual disability and challenging behaviour in integrated work settings: an overview and a model for service provision', *Journal of Intellectual Disability Research*, vol 43, no 1, pp 19–29.

74   Kemp, D. and Carr, E. (1995) 'Reduction of severe problem behaviour in community employment using an hypothesis-driven multicomponent intervention approach', *Journal of the Association for People with Severe Handicaps*, vol 20, pp 239–347.

75   McConkey, R. and Mezza, F. (2001) 'Employment aspirations of people with learning disabilities attending day centres', *Journal of Intellectual Disabilities*, vol 5, no 4, pp 309–318.

76   Rose, J., Saunders, K., Hensel, E. and Kroese, B.S. (2005) 'Factors affecting the likelihood that people with intellectual disabilities will gain employment', *Journal of Intellectual Disabilities*, vol 9, no 1, pp 9–23.

77   Bates, P. (2001) 'The Able Volunteers Programme' (available at www.ndt.org.uk/docsN/able_vols.pdf).

78   Taylor, B.J., McGilloway, S. and Donnelly, M. (2004) 'Preparing young adults with disability for employment', *Health and Community Care in the Community*, vol 12, no 2, pp 93–101.

79   Florian, L., Maudsley, L., Dee, L. and Byers, R. (2000) 'What happens when schooling ends? Further education opportunities for students with profound and complex learning difficulties', *Skill Journal*, vol 67, pp 16–23.

80   Tuckey, L. (2000) 'Barriers to learning faced by adults with learning difficulties and/or disabilities in one estate in Milton Keynes', *Skill Journal*, vol 68, pp 31–32.

81   Boxall, K., Carson, I. and Docherty, D. (2004) 'Room at the academy? People with learning difficulties and higher education', *Disability and Society*, vol 19, no 2, pp 99–112.

82   Jacobsen, Y. and Everrett, G. (2002) *Making the jump: Transition to work. A guide to supporting adults with learning difficulties make the jump from education to employment*, London: Change.

83   Booth, T. and Booth, W. (2003) 'Self-advocacy and supported learning for mothers with learning difficulties', *Journal of Learning Disabilities*, vol 7, no 2, pp 165–193.

84   Lockton, P. (2004) *Final report – Mapping the provision of learning for learners with learning disabilities in Nottingham City and Nottinghamshire*, Nottingham: Marketing Innovation Ltd.

85   Learning and Skills Council (2005) *Through inclusion to excellence* (available at http://readingroom.lsc.gov.uk/Lsc/2005/research/consultation/through-inclusion-to-excellence-summary.pdf).

86   Department for Education and Skills (2005) 'Realising the potential' (available at www.dfes.gov.uk/furthereducation/fereview/finalreport.html).

87   Summers, S.J. and Jones, J. (2004) 'Cross-cultural working in community learning disabilities services: clinical issues, dilemmas and tensions', *Journal of Intellectual Disability Research*, vol 48, no 7, pp 687–694.

88   McIntosh, B. and Whittaker, A. (eds) *Unlocking the future: Developing new lifestyles with people who have complex disabilities*, London: King's Fund.

89   Witcher, S., Stalker, K., Roadburg, M., and Jones, C. (2000) *Direct payments: The impact on choice and control for disabled people*, Edinburgh: Scottish Executive Central Research Unit.

90   Morgan, H. (2001) 'Just good friends?', *Community Living*, vol 14, no 3, pp 20–21, Jan/Feb.

91   Beyer, S. (1995) 'Real jobs and supported employment', in T. Philpot and L. Ward (eds) *Values and visions: Changing ideas in services for people with learning difficulties*, London: Butterworth/Heinemann.

92   Kilsby, M. and Beyer, S. (2001) *Report on the Progress of the Youth Supported Employment Project in England and Wales*, Birmingham: MENCAP.

93   Abbott, D., Townsley, R. and Watson, D. (2003) *Making a difference? Exploring the impact of multi-agency working on disabled children with complex health care needs, their families and the professionals that support them*, Bristol: The Policy Press.

94   Beyer, S., Grove, B., Schneider, J., Simons, K., Williams, V., Heyman, A., Swift, P. and Krijnen-Kemp, E. (2004a) *Working lives: The role of day centres in supporting people with learning disabilities into employment*, DWP, Research Report 203, London: Department for Work and Pensions.

95   Cole, A. and Lloyd, A. (2005) *Shaping the future together: A strategic planning tool for services supporting people with learning disabilities*, London: Foundation for People with Learning Difficulties.

96   DH (Department of Health) (2001) *Valuing People: A new strategy for learning disability for the 21st century*, London: DH.

97   DH (2005) *Independence, well-being and choice: Adult social care Green Paper*, London: DH.

98   FPLD (Foundation for People with Learning Disabilities) (2005) *Identifying and improving mental health support for young people with learning disabilities*, London: FPLD.

99   Gramlich, S., McBride, G. and Snelham, N. with Williams, V. and Simons, K. (2002) *Journey to independence: What self-advocates tell us about direct payments*, Kidderminster: British Institute for Learning Disabilities.

100 McConkey, R. (2004) *Pressures, possibilities and proposals: Northern Ireland review of day services for people with learning disabilities*, Londonderry: University of Ulster.

101 McIntosh, B. and Whittaker, A. (eds) (1998) *Days of change: A practical guide to developing better day opportunities with people with learning difficulties*, London: King's Fund Centre.

102 Mencap (2002) *A life in the day: The modernisation of day services for people with a learning disability*, London: Mencap.

103 Realvoice Media (2005) *Our lives* (DVD and video produced with Wiltshire Social Services).

104 SCIE (Social Care Institute for Excellence) (2005) *Commissioning brief: Knowledge review and analytical report on community-based day activities for people with learning disabilities*, London: SCIE.

105 SCIE (undated) 'Guidelines for preparing a practice survey', SCIE internal document, London: SCIE.

106 Scottish Executive (2000) *The same as you*, Edinburgh: Scottish Executive.

107 Simons, K. and Watson, D. (1999) *New directions? Day services for people with learning disabilities in the 1990's. A review of the research*, Exeter: Centre for Evidence-based Social Services.

108 Swift, P. and Townsley, R. with Cole, A. Lloyd, A. Major, V. Mattingly, M. McIntosh, B. and Williams, V. (2007) *Having a good day? Research review summary*, London: SCIE.

109 Waddilove, D. (2004) *Redesigned and redrawn – Developing new roles in social care,* England: Topss.

110 Welsh Assembly (2001) *Fulfilling the promises,* Cardiff: Welsh Assembly.

111 Williams, V., Abbott, D. and Jefferson, E. (2005) *A taste of independence: An evaluation of Youth PASS and the Youth PASS transition project,* Bristol: West of England Centre for Inclusive Living.

112 McClimmens, A. (2004) 'How the Burton Street project reveals the traditional mould of day swervices', *Learning Disability Practice,* vol 7, part 4, pp 22–23.

113 Logan, E. (2002) 'Springfield education for adults with learning difficulties', *Bristish Journal of Learning Disabilities,* vol 30, no 1, pp 43–46.

Area 1

Brandon Trust
Main contact: Nick Fripp (Development Manager)

Olympus House
Britannia Road
Patchway
Bristol BS34 5TA
nick.fripp@brandontrust.org
www.avon.nhs.uk/mentalhealth/dir/view.asp?item=69

Brandon Trust is a large provider organisation that runs several day centres and residential services in Bristol and the surrounding unitary authorities. It is active in developing new community projects, in which people with learning disabilities are learning and doing things in ordinary settings.

Our team visited a 'nursery project', which was a gardening operation, where people were learning about horticulture, and producing a certain amount of produce which they sell at the local farmers market. We went on to a cafe (Park Cafe), which again is run by people with learning disabilities who are learning about catering, and working towards qualifications. In both these projects, Brandon has linked with local colleges, and is providing qualifications with funding through the Learning and Skills Council (LSC). This is also the case with the Parks Project, in which Brandon took the opportunity to work with the parks and gardens services, and to create a new project within a previously depressed park area. There is now a small group of people with learning disabilities in the centre of this public park, who are working towards certification in park maintenance.

Brandon Trust also operates an individualised support service, and we met two people over lunch who have one-to-one support through

Brandon Trust, and who use their supporters to go out and do things they choose. One of these people had used her supporter to go to bingo, and developed an interest in bingo calling. She now has a paid job to do bingo calling once a week, and her supporter goes along with her.

Area 2

The Orchardville Society
Main contact: Alan Thomson
Commissioner of Services (Department for Employment and Learning)

Lagan Valley Tower
144-145 Ravenhill Road
Belfast BT6 8ED
info@orchardville.com
www.orchardville.com

The Orchardville Society is a medium to large service provider (about 200 service users currently) with a single purpose – to provide vocational training, employment support and career progression for people with learning disabilities. Largely because of parental dissatisfaction with previous centre-based provision, The Orchardville Society was formed some 14 years ago, and parents as well as service users have remained central in its board of management. Orchardville now offers a whole menu of vocational training, job support and employment-related services. There is a strong partnership between the local Trust (commissioner of services) and the Society, and new developments are undertaken through ACET , a networking organisation of several providers and interested parties.

The Society works with schools, in a transition programme that offers every school leaver with a learning disability three job taster experiences. One mother told us how her son had done some office skills as a work taster from school, but had preferred his cafe work. Because of these experiences, he was entering adult life with a chosen pathway into work. Orchardville has a training office (basic office skills training, using contract work), an employment support service (with job assessment, job matching and coaching), and other training units (for example, two cafes). The organisation also works with employers, to ensure good relationships and a good supply of jobs.

One very strong message was that people with learning disabilities should have 'careers', not just 'jobs'. Orchardville therefore continues with support and offers of progression, so that people can move on. This is how the commissioner put it: 'If life is an archipelago of islands, Orchardville is a bridge from one place to another'.

Area 3

Promoting Independence Project
Main contact: Alison Shepherd (Community Services Manager)

c/o Trinity Fields School
Caerphilly Road
Ystrad Mynach
Caerphilly CF82 7XW
shepa@caerphilly.gov.uk
www.caerphilly.gov.uk/newsandviews/news/pressrelease/0900-0999/
0954.htm

Promoting Independence is a partnership initiative, which for the first two years of its life was funded solely by the European Social Fund. The lead partner is Trinity Fields School and Resource Centre, and other partners include the Mencap-supported employment service, the health and occupational therapy service, the county inclusion services, and the community education service. The project supports young people to develop a person-centred plan, and to identify things they want to do in their lives. Young people then obtain support and training to enable them to develop a range of skills for their adult life, along five pathways – employment, independent living, social inclusion (leisure), independent relationships and inclusive or continuing education. The partnership approach has worked well, because the various agencies all 'own' their part of the project, and are able to bring their own skills and ideas to it. For instance, the occupational therapist has had an important role in offering transport training to young people.

The project includes job coaching, and we met young people who had obtained paid employment and were delighted by that outcome.

Parents also were very involved in person-centred planning and in the outcomes for their son or daughter. The work is totally individualised and community based – for instance, one young person we visited had had a work placement in a pub. His job coach got to know him quite well, and responded to his wish to learn about DJ work. He found him an opportunity to attend a community technology centre, and we were able to visit him there while he learnt the skills to become a DJ.

Area 4

North Lanarkshire
Main contact: Morag Dendy

DendyM@northlan.gov.uk
www.northlan.gov.uk/caring+for+you/learning+disability/
day+opportunities/learning+disabilities+day+opportunities.html

North Lanarkshire is a good example of a whole local authority strategy in action, with a strong leadership and values base. The five day centres in the area have now become 'locality bases', and are moving over rapidly into providing community support, instead of centre-based provision. At the same time, some 300 people have recently left long-stay institutions, and are now receiving individualised services for supported living, and have their own tenancies or homes. North Lanarkshire works with a large number of providers, who work together and share their experience, rather than competing with each other. In this area, there is no division between support for living and support for day activities. Because of this, people with learning disabilities are having true individualised support, with supporters they know and trust.

North Lanarkshire also provides supported employment services, both through the council (former day centre staff have moved over successfully into supported employment) and also within its provider services. 110 people with learning difficulties have real paid jobs, and all of these are over 16 hours a week. Others are starting up micro-enterprises. One person we met has a business in car washing, and another is planning to start up a cafe. Everything is based on a person-centred model, with person-centred plans for all service users and a high emphasis on accessible information and the use of multi-media at every level.

One parent of a young man with high support needs told us about how she had initially been very concerned about day centre closure. With other parents, she had taken part in active protests. However, her son now takes part in a one-to-one community based support service, for six young men with complex needs. This runs from their own homes, and they go out to different places with their supporters, who work closely with parents and family members in a person-centred way. This parent has been totally won over to the new model.

Area 5

Thurrock
Main contact: Neil Woodbridge (Service manager for Community Services)

13-15 Clarence Rd
Grays
Essex RM17 6QA
Tel: 01375 413707
nwoodbridge@thurrock.gov.uk

Thurrock is a local authority area that has started to modernise its day services, by moving from large day centres into smaller community bases. The new approach is explicitly based on the social model of disability, and so the role of support services is quite explicitly to overcome those barriers. There is a resource forum, where people can obtain information about what is available and things they may want to do in the community. They also have a supported employment service, and community mapping. The job descriptions of staff who formerly worked in day centres have been changed, and they have moved over into new roles as community facilitators or even personal assistants for those who need one-to-one support to get out and about. Up to 19 people each day can have this service, and the plan is to link this with the development of direct payments in the area. Basildon and Thurrock Independent Advocacy Service (BATIAS), a local self-advocacy organisation, is paid to give an independent view on how people with higher needs are being included.

One cohesive group of self-advocates has developed its own organisation, and they are provided with a building. They run their own leisure and other activities. Thurrock has a vision to back up its services, and that vision is about handing over power. One of the aspects of that vision is that people with learning disabilities will be directors of their own 'community interest' company, and that people will be able to buy in services from that company with their direct payments.

Area 6

Pure Innovations Ltd
Main contact: Doug Cresswell (Chief Executive)

Sanderling Building
Bird Hall Lane
Cheadle Heath
Stockport SK3 0RF
Tel: 0161 474 5900
Doug.cresswell@pureinnovations.co.uk

Arising from 19 years' of experience of getting people into *real* jobs through a 'Work Link' programme, Pure Innovations has formed itself into an independent company and broken away from local authority provision. They continue to develop people's skills to empower them to gain greater independence, and provide alternatives to day services – both through volunteering projects (such as cafes, setting up a community radio station with a radio marketing team and a park warden service) and through real, paid jobs. People with high support needs are in paid employment at John Lewis and at the BBC. During 2004, the team placed 30 people into employment and supported 130 who were already in work. The scheme includes many people with high support needs or profound learning disabilities, and will find them jobs that match their needs and interests, perhaps for a few hours each week.

Pure Innovations has created a new way of delivering supported employment through 'Embracing Diversity', which brings together large employers and works strategically and supportively with them to employ people from many different under-represented groups.

Area 7

London Borough of Newham, NuLife Day and Employment Opportunities
Main contact: Jackie Brooks (Day Opportunities and Employment Manager)

St Marks Community Centre
Tollgate Road
Beckton
London E6 5YA
Tel: 020 7474 4888
jackie.brooks@newham.gov.uk

NuLife is a service that supports adults with learning disabilities to develop person-centred plans, and to achieve their goals in a variety of individualised ways in the community. The service developed from the reprovision of two large day centres to form six community teams operating from ordinary community centres around the borough. Activities, opportunities and services are planned according to people's expressed wishes through person-centred planning approaches often making use of multi-media to capture people's choices. NuLife also supports several people with autism and challenging behaviour to have individual services from their homes, rather than accessing the community bases.

Some individuals with learning disabilities receive one-to-one support, through NuLife, and are often involved in choosing their own staff. This results in a more flexible arrangement, so that their chosen activities are not necessarily limited to the 9-5 model.

Newham was part of Changing Days II and this was the catalyst to Newham investing in a circles facilitator post, a community capacity builder post and a person-centred planning coordinator – not just with a focus on day opportunities. There is a focus on community development across services and service users have been involved in developing community directories, doing access audits at a new leisure centre and delivering disability training for public bus drivers.

The employment strategy is looking to increase employment opportunities for people with a range of needs. The supported employment service, First Line, was established in 1999 as part of the day service changes. It has grown by accessing external funding and through part-nership arrangements. It has supported around 130 people into paid work (around 25-30 per year more recently). Another employment service runs a catering service, gardening, maintenance work and they undertake pre- work assessments/preparation to enable progression into supported employment.

Area 8

Community Support Team, Norfolk County Council
Main contact: Sarah Stock (Manager Community Support Team)

Level Two
Carrow Hse
301 Kings St
Norwich NR1 2TN
Sarah.Stock@norfolk.gov.uk

The service was set up for people leaving Little Plumstead Hospital and is county-wide with offices based in the Norwich area. They provide a non-building-based service, supporting people one to one. There are support workers across Norfolk, answerable to team leaders and coordi-nators, and one of the strong features of this service is the person-centred values base that is shared and actioned at every level, from the County manager to the personal support workers.

Most people in the service have high support needs, and each person's service is individually commissioned. Each person is helped to participate in community organisations, to develop friendships, achieve greater independence and community inclusion. Currently, 88 people across the county are using these individualised support services, 33 of these are young school leavers in the east, and another 8 are currently referred. They have on average three days of support per week. The support workers work with people from their own homes, and there is no large building base. They work closely with staff in small homes, parents and families, to ensure that there is a truly person-centred approach to planning and developing people's activities and lives.

Very much in the spirit of the person-centred model, time is spent in getting to know each person, and there is a high degree of respect given to people with learning disabilities as choice makers. This is evident, for instance, in one example where a team of staff had been on lifeguard training in order to enable a woman with challenging behaviour to go swimming. About 30% of people being supported have their own car as they are recipients of the higher level of Mobility Allowance. Support workers are personal drivers for the people they support, and there are no large vehicles or buses in the service.

Contacts for services included in this report

Page	Area	Contact	Example of...	Comment
45	South Gloucestershire	**Kathy Mackay** Head of Joint Learning Disabilities Service Tel: 01454 866343 Kathy.Mackay@southglos.gov.uk	Achieving integrated leisure opportunities	Also a first-wave in-control pilot site
47	Linkage Green, Mablethorpe	**Shelagh Price** Manager, Linkage Green Tel: 01507 479305 bowlinggreen@freeuk.com (or Pauline Gibson, Operations Mngr)	Community-based social enterprise involving people with higher support needs	
48 & 64	Norfolk	**Marcia Derbyshire** Project Manager Tel: 01603 481139 marcia.derbyshire@norfolk.gov.uk	Development of FE provision related to social enterprises and self-employment	Developing innovative 'skills for the job' curriculum accessing mainstream courses

Page	Area	Contact	Example of...	Comment
49	Fife EmployAbility Team: Aspire. Fife, Scotland	**Jill Morris** EmployAbility: Aspire Tel: 01592 416414 Jill.Morris@fife.gov.uk www.fifeadultdayservices.org.uk	Supported Employment Scheme providing a targeted service for people with higher functioning autistic spectrum disorder or Asperger's syndrome	
50	Weavers Restaurant Trust Bethnal Green, East London	**Aruna Sharma** Weavers Restaurant Trust Tel: 0207 729 3111 aruna@wrtrust.org.uk	Accredited training for work in hospitality and catering, IT and adult literacy. Open to everyone. Job-seeking support built in	
51	Stratford, Warwickshire	**Sue Courtney** Day Service Manager Tel: 01789 269178 Sue.courtney@warwickshire.gov.uk	Managing staff time to achieve evening support	Also hiring out rooms at reduced rate to community groups in exchange for free places

Page	Area	Contact	Example of...	Comment
53	Grapevine, Coventry	**Clare Wightman** Director, Grapevine Tel: 02476 631041 grapevine.the@talk21.com	People with learning disabilities in leading positions, with control over developments	Also community connecting work for example, community activities hosted by Grapevine as step to integration, community integration, summer litter picks, summer festival and arts events
54	WISE, South Wales	**Kaynie McClellan** Director, WISE Tel: 01792 538538 admin@wisewales.org.uk	Family involvement in developing supported employment	Also project working with young people with learning disabilities in final year of school
55	Mencap, Northern Ireland	**Louise McQuillan** Mencap, Northern Ireland Tel: 02890 492666 louise.mcquillan@mencap.org.uk	People with learning disabilities working in paid positions with power and influence	

Page	Area	Contact	Example of...	Comment
56	Listening To Us, Essex	**Ryan Jones** Service Manager Listening to Us Tel: 01245 392050/ 392051 ListeningToUs@mencap. org.uk	People with learning disabilities working in paid positions with power and influence	
56	Birmingham People First, West Midlands	**Birmingham People First** Tel: 0121 678 8857 pf@bvsc.org	Mystery shopping	
57	Alumwell Project Walsall	**Karen Garbutt** Day Service Modernisation Manager, Walsall MBC Tel: 01922 636215 garbuttk@walsall.gov.uk	Partnership with Resident's Association to develop a community centre open to all	
57 & 78	Maidenhead and Windsor	**Cindy Blackman** Windsor and Maidenhead Day Services Manager Tel: 01753 833654	Creation of multi-sensory room and accessible changing facilities at leisure centre, for benefit of all community	Also, partnership with local girls school to develop a buddy scheme

Page	Area	Contact	Example of...	Comment
58	Leicester	**Chris Ainge** Leicester City Council Tel: 0116 221 2732 Chris.ainge@leic.gov.uk	Commissioning of a Sikh community association to provide a service for people with learning disabilities	
59	Shropshire	**Adrian Johnson** Operations Manager for Adults with learning difficulties? Community services Shropshire County Council Tel: 01743 254003 adrian.johnson@shropshire-cc.gov.uk	Use of local authority capital funding to achieve community bases and accessible changing places	A large rural area
61	Hounslow, West London	**Nicky Bitar** Tel: 0208 321 3588 nicky.bitar@hounslow.gov.uk	People with learning disabilities employed as travel buddies for other people with learning disabilities	

Page	Area	Contact	Example of...	Comment
61	Positive Futures Team Nottingham	**Jim Broughton** Easy Information coordinator Tel: 0115 934 9566 info@ pfhlc.org.uk	People with learning disabilities producing easy read information	
62	Better Days, Newcastle	**Lesley Mountain** Better Days Tel: 0191 281 5541 better-days@lineone.net	People with learning disabilities training staff in community settings & services	
64	Leicestershire Adult Learning Service Transitions Project	**Alison Doggett** Leicestershire City Council Tel:0116 267 0042 adoggett@leics.gov.uk	Adult community learning opened up for people with high support needs	
66	Nottingham City	**Martin Jackaman** Day Service Modernisation Manager, Nottingham City Tel: 0115 915 1077 Martin.Jackaman@nottin ghamcity.gov.uk	Development of accessible changing places in community spaces	

Page	Area	Contact	Example of...	Comment
66	Pedal Power Cardiff, Wales	**Sybil Williams** Manager, Pedal Power Tel: 07974 121464 Sybil.Williams@bromor-tr.wales.nhs.uk	Role of health staff in developing healthy living leisure opportunities	
67	Dewsbury, West Yorks	**Darren O'Donovan** SW Yorks Mental Health Trust Tel: 01924 816274 Darren.ODonovan@midyorks.nhs.uk	Role of health staff in developing healthy living leisure opportunities	
68	EMAPP, Ealing and Hounslow, West London	**Alka Tripathi** Ruhi Grover or Muna Dhiriya EMAPP Tel: 0208 232 1595 Alka.tripathi@mencap.org.uk	Advocacy for people from black and minority ethnic communties – developing into day activities	

Page	Area	Contact	Example of...	Comment
68 & 87	Waltham Forest, East London	**Kalwant Panesar** Community Day Services Manager Waltham Forest Tel: 0208 496 2706 Kalwant.panesar@waltha mforest.gov.uk	Community day service for Asian women	Monitoring of community-based support
69	Options for Life, Sandwell, West Midlands	**Mark Sturgeon** Day Services Manager, Options for Life Tel: 0121 544 6611 Mark.sturgeon@optionsf orlife.info	Community day service for Asian women	
75	HILT, Hackney, East London	**John Cahill** HILT Tel: 0208 985 5511 john@hilt.org.uk	Use of multi-media to enhance communication and individualised planning	
76	Inclusion, Glasgow	**Francis Brown** Inclusion Glasgow Tel: 0141 427 5577 Francis.brown@inclusion-glasgow.org	Integrated whole-life approach based on person-centered planning	

Page	Area	Contact	Example of...	Comment
76	Ling Trust, Essex	**Maureen Cook** Ling Trust, Essex Tel: 01206 767287 maureen.cook@talk21.com	Integrated whole-life approach based on person-centered planning	
76	Partners for Inclusion, Ayrshire	**Doreen Kelly** Director Tel: 01563 825555 Doreen.Kelly@Partnersfor Inclusion.org	Integrated whole-life approach based on person-centered planning	
76	New Avenues, Newham, East London	**Kim Foo** Tel: 020 8502 3933 (main office number) Kim.foo@heritagecare.co.uk	Move from centre focus to home focused support, and management of the process	
82 & 84	Garstang Deanery Project, Scotforth, Lancs	**Sheron Hall** Coordinator, Garstang Deanery Project Tel: 01524 843135 sheron.hall@bsrgrassroots.org	Partnership with Blackburn diocese to provide individualised community opportunities	

Page	Area	Contact	Example of...	Comment
82	Southampton	**Sue Harris** Manager, Southampton Day Services, Southampton City Council Tel: 023 8083 4608 sue.harris@southampton .gov.uk	Partnership with Sport England to develop community centre for use by all	
384	Chester, Ellesmere Port and Neston	**Sandra Johnson** Health Promotion Practitioner (Learning Disabilities) Cheshire and Wirral Partnership NHS Trust Tel: 01244 364670 sandra.johnson@cwpnt. nhs.uk	Partnership work with borough's active communities officer	

Page	Area	Contact	Example of...	Comment
84	Cheshire	**Jane Stanley-McCrave** Welfare to Work Lead, Cheshire County Council Tel: 01606 835286 jane.mccrave@cheshire.gov.uk	Partnerships to deliver employment experiences for young people in transition	'Positive Awards for Business' annual awards
85	Poole	**Philip Mason** Adult Social Service, Borough of Poole Tel: 01202 261017 p.mason@poole.gov.uk	Partnership between Supported Employment Service and local Jobcentre Plus	
85	Wellington Community Enablement Project, Somerset	**Sally Hill** Community Enablement Project and CHI Centre Tel: 01823 665506 sallyhill@talk21chinternational.org.uk.com or David Waddilove, Skills for Care England	Community development through community cafe concept, and development of new staff roles	
86	Shaw Trust, Bromley	**Amanda Lewis** Projects Manager Tel: 0208 998 0067	Transfer of staff into new organisation and roles	

Other services with helpful learning from community-based practice...

Sabre Employment, South London: supported employment provider
www.sabre-employment.co.uk

A Chance to Work Project, Barnardos: supported employment for young people
www.barnardos.org.uk/achancetowork

Independent Day Service, York: community-based service for people presenting challenging behaviours
Tel: 01904 724185

Quest Supported Employment Agency, Innovate Trust, South Glamorgan, Wales:supported employment provider
www.innovate-trust.org.uk/Quest.htm

Enable Scotland: various supported employment projects and schemes
Tel: 0141 225 1651

Progress Recruitment, Blackpool: supported employment provider
Tel: 01253 477818

Action on Disabilities Project, Upper Springfield Development Trust, Belfast, Northern Ireland – community inclusion work
Tel: 02890 236677

Wokingham District Council day services: reflective approach to the modernisation of three day centres
Tel: 0118 979 2588

Generate, South London: variety of projects around social life, friendships, employment, speaking up
Tel: 0208 879 6333

Focus Individualised Support (Circles Network), Bristol: person-centred community inclusion work, open to people with challenging behaviours and/or profound and complex impairments
Tel: 0117 373 7010

Other services that were especially recommended, but could not be contacted...

The Life Options Project, SCOVO, Carmarthenshire, Wales: transition planning and support
www.scovo.org.uk

Credo East (Circles Network): supporting young people with multiple impairments in planning and looking forward to adult life
www.circlesnetwork.org.uk/credo.htm

Local authority day service, Marshfield, Herefordshire: modernised day service with work focus, including micro enterprise developments
Tel: 01568 614772

Useful resources

PAMIS (Promoting a More Inclusive Society) Changing Places campaign: to highlight the inadequacies of current provision and ensure that toilets for disabled people are made fully accessible that is, with sufficient space, privacy and appropriate equipment (height-adjustable bench and hoist) to allow carers to change people in dignified and hygienic conditions without endangering their own health
www.dundee.ac.uk/pamis

The 'Inclusion Web': a tool for mapping and tracking inclusion
www.ndt.org.uk

The Micro-Enterprise Development Network: An email discussion forum supported by web pages
www.ndt.org.uk

Social Inclusion Planner: a free software package to help people plan and support social inclusion, available from the national development team, with supporting training
www.ndt.org.uk

The Choice Forum: an interactive discussion site, good for posting queries and networking
www.fpld.org.uk

The Disabled Workers Cooperative: hosts an online database of the skills, products and services that disabled people can offer, and a portal where you can search for employees and advertise vacancies for free
www.disabledworkers.org.uk

Transport for London Travel Assistance Scheme: offers the services of a travel buddy to help someone develop the confidence and skills to make a journey on their own
www.tfl.gov.uk/dial-a-ride/travel-assistance.shtml

Travel Training good practice guidance, June 2005, produced by Public Transport for Greater Manchester
www.gmpte.com

Acting Up: multimedia work with people who have communication difficulties
www.acting-up.org.uk

The 'in-control' development sites, learning from the implementation of individualised funding
www.in-control.org.uk

John McKnight's work on community development and community building
www.northwestern.edu/ipr/people/mcknight.html

ADEPT Community Development Agency
3 Market Way
Coventry CV1 1DF
Tel: 024 7623 0606
e-mail: info@adept.org.uk

Scottish Community Development Centre (Glasgow): a useful source
of information and ideas about community development
Tel: 0141 248 1924
www.scdc.org.uk

Community Development Foundation (London): anything and
everything to do with community development
Tel: 020 7833 1772
www.cdf.org.uk

Community Development Xchange: another helpful source of information and ideas, and for networking, links to other helpful websites
www.cdx.org.uk

Books and other publications

Bates, P. *On supported volunteering: A real asset*, available from the
NDT
www.ndt.org.uk

Duffy, S. (2006) O*n supporting people to achieve full citizenship. Keys
to citizenship 2: A guide to getting good support for people with learning
disabilities*, Paradigm

The Elfrida Society, *Community Living*, quarterly publication focused
on people with learning disabilities achieving equal citizenship
Tel: 0207 359 7443

Living Well, quarterly publication focused on practical examples of how people with learning disabilities are being supported to achieve employment, learning and leisure, Pavilion Publishing, Tel: 01273 623222

Community Development Journal, Quarterly publication reporting research and practice in community development worldwide, Oxford University Press
http://cdj.oxfordjournals.org or www.oxfordjournals.org

The Journal of Community Work and Development, bi-annual publication, available from the Scottish Community Development Centre Tel: 0141 248 1924

Community Connecting, web-based publication
www.communityconnecting.co.uk

Index